FERNS
FOR THE HOME AND GARDEN

FERNS
FOR THE HOME AND GARDEN

Gillean Dunk

ANGUS
& ROBERTSON
PUBLISHERS

ANGUS & ROBERTSON PUBLISHERS

Unit 4, Eden Park, 31 Waterloo Road,
North Ryde, NSW, Australia 2113, and
16 Golden Square, London W1R 4BN,
United Kingdom

First published in Australia
by Angus & Robertson Publishers in 1982
First published in the United Kingdom
by Angus & Robertson UK in 1982
Reprinted 1983, 1984, 1986, 1987

Copyright © Gillean Dunk 1982

National Library of Australia
Cataloguing-in-publication data.

Dunk, Gillean.
  Ferns for the home and garden.

  Bibliography.
  Includes Index.
  ISBN 0 207 14675 6.

  1. Ferns, Ornamental. I. Title.

635. 9' 3731

Designed by Lynda Christie
Typeset in 11pt Tiffany by Setrite Typesetters
Printed in Singapore

CONTENTS

FOREWORD

Until a few years ago I ran a small nursery. The lovely plants which stocked the shop brightened my working days there, and, I think, the feelings of the people who came to buy. The seasons and flowers came and went—potted bulbs in spring, cool daisies in the hot months of summer, golden maples in autumn, and primroses and polyanthus to brighten the grey winter days; but no matter the time of year, there were always ferns and they always looked wonderful.

Everyone admired them and almost everyone bought one, but I always felt anxious as each one left the shop for I had come to realise in the time that I was in business that few people knew how to care for them. There has always been so little information about their cultivation—a few paragraphs or a small chapter in a "complete" garden book, or a detailed description of spore and frond put together by a dedicated botanist was all that I could ever find. Magazine articles were inaccurate and misleading and growers, though helpful, were out of touch with the problems that indoor growing and small-time gardening present.

So this book about the care of the beautiful fern will, I hope, make the would-be grower confident and the long-time grower keen to grow more. The fern has a long history of association with man, a lot of it fanciful, some of it useful and all of it interesting, so I hope, too, that the book will entertain as well as inform.

Several people have helped me with *Ferns for the Home and Garden*.

I am especially grateful to Chris Goudey of Lara, Victoria, whose time, patience, and seemingly infinite knowledge of ferns have added greatly to its authority and scope. Most of the ferns in the colour plates are from his nursery.

I am also very grateful to Gordon Ling of Warburton, Victoria, who generously made his collection of old books available to me so that I was able to include interesting facts about the fern's history and usage, and reproductions of charming Victorian prints.

I am greatly indebted to my photographer, John Squire of Melbourne, whose skill with lens and light made the words come to life.

I wish to express my thanks to Tony Hitchin, the editor of *Home Beautiful* who lent me the modern interior and courtyard garden photographs from the magazine's files.

I wish to thank, too, the Hawthorn Arts Council, of Melbourne, for the use of its exhibition of Victorian interiors, and Bone's Nursery of Berwick, Victoria, for the use of valuable stock plants to grace those interiors.

And my special thanks to Brian Lee for valued help with geographical research.

Gillean Dunk
September 1981

FERNS—AN INTRODUCTION
1

Today's fern forest is almost a primeval place. Except for the scale of the plants, a rainforest dominated by ferns is very similar to the forests of millions of years ago when dinosaurs roamed the earth, mountains erupted and seas lay over the continents' deserts. Most of the land was swamp where giant horsetails towered as high as ten-storey buildings and clubmosses grew almost as high, spreading their huge fronds over the ferns beneath. The ferns, giants too compared to today's plants, spread their lush and finely divided leaves wide to catch the little light that filtered through the canopy formed by their enormous cousins above them. Under the ferns lay the steaming earth clothed in the earliest forms of plant life, the mosses and lichens.

All must have been quiet for no insects buzzed and whirred through the air and no birds or mammals called to each other from the branches overhead. Everything was green and gloomy—no flowering plants declared their presence in the shades of the rainbow and no birds flashed by in bright plumage. This was the Carboniferous Age, some 350,000,000 years ago—the time of the fern and its allies.

The climate then was much milder than it is today. The world was shrouded in mists and rain was almost constant. In this warm, moist atmosphere the ancient fern-type plants thrived and grew to giant proportions, dominating the landscape with their strange shapes.

Towards the end of the Carboniferous Age the world's climate changed and conditions were not as congenial for these huge plants. Many of the watery places dried and were situated further apart so that the plants' reproduction, dependent as it was on water, was not as prolific. The mists cleared and the appearance of the vegetation changed too; leaves did not have to be as big to capture light vital for life energy and so smaller plants evolved. Competition from the new, sophisticated seed bearing plants, the conifers, pines and their relations which could reproduce without water, became stronger. The horsetails and clubmosses succumbed to the new atmosphere, fell, rotted and became the coal

seams of today, and the ferns were driven into the areas where the conditions of their beginnings still existed—the swamps, stream edges and moisture-laden mountain sides.

By the time of the Mesozoic era, which began about 225,000,000 years ago, the modern fern families with their characteristic fiddleheads and acropetal growth (that is, the maturing of the leaf tissues from the base towards the tip), were well established. Fossil records of this time show the existence of several families including Marattiaceae, Osmundaceae, Gleicheniaceae and Schizeaeceae, some individual species of which are alive and flourishing today. Ferns may actually have existed before the Carboniferous time as fossils from the earlier Devonian era, some 395,000,000 years ago, show vegetation with fern-like characteristics. These remains are thought to be of plants that are now extinct and are regarded as the ancestors of the "seed" ferns, which may have been the first seed bearing plants, and our modern fern species. A few of what are called "primitive" ferns, like the species of *Angiopteris* and *Psilophyton*, are still with us today as living fossils.

In all this time to the present day the true ferns have become smaller and more complex, but their method of reproduction has not changed and, like their allies, they have remained dependent on water to recreate themselves and have thereby retained a link with their ancestors, the first of the vascular plants, the seaweeds and mosses.

Today ferns are found in almost every country of the world and ferns from the same family are found in many different and far apart countries—the species may vary slightly or much, but the family or mother group is the same. This wide distribution of individual species of a genus, which is wider than any in the flowering-plant world, is thought by botanists to be related to the fern's ability to disperse its dust-like spores. Wind and water have carried the minute particles to all parts of the world and there, if the essential moisture is present, the spores have germinated—perhaps thousands of kilometres from the parent plant. The *Nephrolepis* genus is an interesting example—its thirty or so species can be found in every continent of the world. On a smaller scale, dispersal patterns within a continent have been related to prevailing winds. *Asplenium septentrionale*, a widespread fern in the western United States, is also found growing in small pockets in mountain areas in the east.

Though we usually think of ferns as essentially plants of shaded, damp forests of the temperate and tropical parts of the world, they have adapted to a surprising number and different types of habitats. In tropical rainforests their myriad varieties dominate the vegetation. Their numbers decrease with increasing latitude and altitude and decreasing moisture and humidity so that there are fewer varieties and numbers in warm temperate areas than in tropical areas and fewer still in cool temperate areas where the atmosphere tends to be drier. They can be found in the crevices of coastal cliffs where they tolerate constant washing with salt spray and in arid, exposed heathlands and dry rocky outcrops where shade, water and humus-rich soil are scarce. Some survive in subalpine areas covered by winter snow for months each year and some appear to thrive in cracks and crevices of city buildings where they are happily tolerant of pollution and full sun.

In their varying environments ferns have adapted themselves for survival. Some terrestrials, like species of the *Lygodium* genus, climb so that they can reach the light, others like the tree ferns, *Cyathea* and *Dicksonia*, have developed tall trunks and huge spreading fronds so that they can have their share of the light. Epiphytes like the *Platycerium* have developed nest-like leaves to catch falling vegetation and turn it into humus and a readily available plant food—this high up in the tree tops where they dwell.

A few ferns, like some of the species of *Doryopteris* and *Cheilanthes* have developed unique mechanisms which enable them to withstand long periods of drought. Their usually small, tough fronds are covered by minute hairs giving them a silvery or woolly appearance and protecting the plant against strong sunlight and moisture loss. Plants with these characteristics are the xerophytes of the fern world.

Aquatic ferns such as *Azolla*, and semi-aquatics such as *Marsilea* have developed small scale-like or clover shaped fronds which enable them to float on the water's surface. In its watery environment the *Marsilea* has also made an evolutionary leap by developing a more advanced reproduction mechanism than any other fern (see page 122).

The filmy ferns, for example the *Hymenophyllum* and *Trichomanes*, have hardly any structure to their fronds at all so that the delicate one-cell thick tissues can absorb water directly from the moisture-laden air of their natural habitats. Other fern species have developed interesting survival mechanisms which are all their own. For example, *Polypodium bifrons* has water-storing sacs for times of drought and *Nephrolepis cordifolia* var. *tuberosa* has developed food storing tubers.

Classification

The plant kingdom is divided into two main groups—Phanerogams, the seed bearing plants, and Cryptogams, the non-seed bearing plants. Ferns belong to the Cryptogam group. The two great sub-kingdoms are divided into classes, orders, families, genera and species. It is interesting to look at some of these divisions because through them we can see the evolution of plant life and trace reasons for a particular plant's dominance or survival.

The Cryptogams are divided into three:

The Thallophyts, a group of about 125,000 species of the most primitive plants found on earth—the algae and the fungi.

The Bryophyts, a group of about 20,000 species of mosses and liverworts. These are a little more sophisticated in that they have a hair-like appendage known as a rhizoid which anchors the plant to the ground and absorbs water with a capillary-like action. The rhizoid, though, is not a true root as it cannot absorb nutrients.

The Pteridophytes, a group of about 10,000 species to which true ferns and their allies belong. While there are many different forms within this group, all reproduce by means of spores and all are true vascular plants. Vascular plants are those which contain bundles of vein tissue which carry water and nutrient to all parts of the plant and give rigidity and the ability to grow erect. Thus this group represents a major evolutionary advance.

Four divisions of the Pteridophytes group reflect further evolutionary advances from the primitive plant forms of the Psilotinae division (fork ferns) through the Lycopodinae division (clubmosses and selanginellas and quillworts) and Sphenopsida class (horsetails) to the most sophisticated and, in evolutionary terms, most recently developed Filicineae class, the class to which all true ferns belong.

Further divisions into orders and families, genera and species thereafter reflect the smaller, more subtle changes that ferns have made in adapting themselves to their own ecological environments—changes in habitats such as from water to land, changes in structure of the rhizome or stem, for example whether it creeps or stands erect, or of the leaves such as shape and venation, and changes in habits of growth such as whether they are epiphytic, or terrestrial, climbing or crawling. But the major characteristic by which ferns (and all plants) are classified is based on the means by which the species reproduces and the structure of the reproductive parts. In seed bearing plants such distinctions are generally more conspicuous; in ferns the structure and positioning of the tiny spore bearing parts is perhaps less obvious but is important and can explain why a species of a genus may differ in frond shape and mode of growth from all other species of the same genus.

The structure of ferns

Though it is not the purpose of this book to provide a strict botanical description by which ferns can be identified, some introduction to their specialised structure is essential. Ferns are a unique group of plants and there is a unique set of botanical terms to describe them.

What is called the stem in other plants, that is, the part which is leaf bearing on top and root producing on the bottom, is referred to as the *rhizome*. In ferns the rhizome can creep above or under the ground, or climb, or it can grow erect. When it forms a trunk, as in tree ferns, it is called a *caudex*.

From the rhizome or caudex emerge the leaves or fronds and it is a characteristic of all but one fern family (the Ophioglossalceae containing the *Ophioglossum* and *Botrychium* genera) that the young fronds are curled up and unroll as they grow.

The fronds of ferns may be undivided (simple), divided (compound) or much divided (decompound). The lower part of the stalk, from the rhizome to the base of the leaf blade or *lamina* is called a *stipe*. Beyond this, where it forms the midrib of fronds, it is called a *rachis*. A branch from the rachis, as in divided fronds, is called a *secondary rachis* and, if there is a further branching from the secondary rachis this is called a *tertiary rachis*.

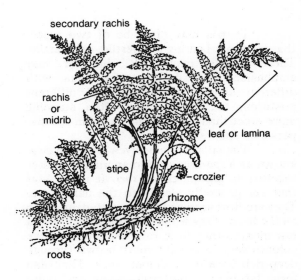

Generalised fern sporophyte

There are two types of lamina structure. One is composed of *lobes* where the divisions of the lamina do not extend to the rachis. The other is composed of *pinnae*, the small leaflets formed when the lamina divisions do reach the rachis. If a pinna itself is divided into yet smaller segments, these are called *pinnules*.

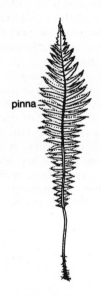

Leaf shapes: a divided or compound frond

Fronds may often be of two types, that is, spore bearing and fertile, or infertile. These fronds may look alike or may emphasise their different functions with different shapes (*dimorphic*) and different postures, the fertile frond often standing more erect than the infertile to aid in the dispersal of spores.

The spores themselves form in a case known as a *sporangium* and sporangia cluster together in groups called *sori*. It is the sori that are generally visible to the naked eye. They are first seen as light green indentations on the back of the fronds. As they ripen over a few months they form raised clusters whose colours vary from light rusty brown through deep rich browns to almost black. They also form fascinating patterns—some are quite random dots or lines, some are precise, some

form bands of felt ribbons around the perimeter of the pinna while others lie along the main veins and some cover the entire undersurface of the pinna. The sori may be covered by a thin membrane called an *indusium* or the margin of the leaf may be rolled over to protect those that form on the edge. This rolled portion of the leaf is called a *false indusium*. As the sori mature the indusium shrinks and is eventually shed when the spore cases are ready to open and release the spores.

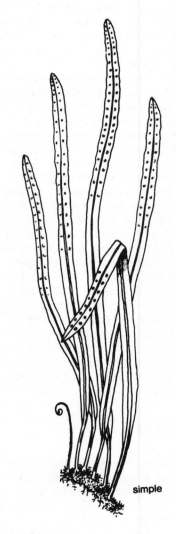

An undivided or simple frond

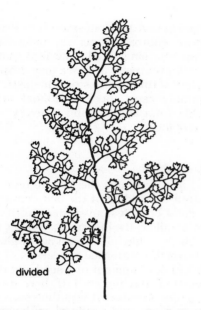

A maidenhair fern frond is an example of a much divided or decompound frond

The sporangia can be seen easily with a hand lens. They are rounded or egg shaped capsules on incredibly delicate stalks. Each capsule is banded or in some cases marked by a ring of cells of a much tougher consistency than those that make up the spore cases. This ring of cells, called an *annulus*, contracts and tears at a certain stage of dehydration and thus opens the spore case and releases the mature spores. The opening action is actually explosive and the spores are literally flung out of the case. There may be several dozen sporangia in each cluster and each produces an even number of spores, usually sixty-four, so the total number of spores produced by a fern in each life cycle can be counted in millions.

The spores are like dust and it is impossible to see their structure without a high-powered magnifying glass. Close up they are bean shaped or pyramid shaped according to species and vary in colour from green to

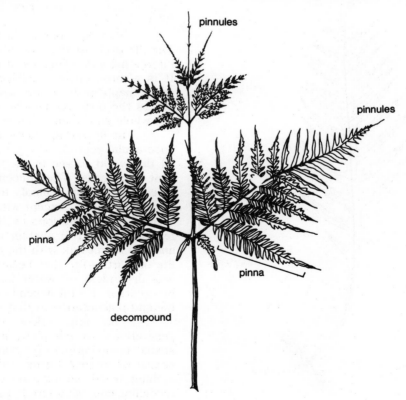

The decompound frond of a bracken fern

Two examples of a lobed frond

black and in texture from smooth to wrinkled. Some are spotted, some are plain. All are made up of a single cell. The fern that each spore will eventually produce may grow to be the size of a tuft of grass or a majestic palm, but initially each spore is almost indistinguishable from another and in every case is microscopic.

Life cycle

The fern and the way it reproduced was, until the middle of the last century, one of the great botanical mysteries. Nothing was known at all of its life cycle, though it was assumed that, like all other known plants, it went through the normal processes of fertilisation and development of a seed and thence, regeneration. But the seed (if there was such a thing) was invisible. It was thus surrounded by superstition and credited with supernatural properties because of this seemingly magical ability to re-create itself. (See page 27.)

Magical it is not but fascinating it is. The life cycle of the fern is one of the most interesting and intriguing of the plant world. It is a most ancient and primitive process which happens in a very low key way, and unless the observer knows what to look for the whole show can be missed.

In flowering plants the complicated spectacular reproductive process is there for all the world to see in the form of flowers, fruit and seeds. They depend on the wind, insects, birds and animals for their procreation, all of which, except wind of course, are relatively new additions to life on earth. The fern's reproductive system is much simpler and is a direct link with the earliest forms of life on earth—life that began in the sea and was dependent on water for its energy and procreation. It still depends on water for its life and regeneration of that life.

The fern takes two alternating generations to complete its life cycle: a sexual (*gametophyte*) generation and a non-sexual (*sporophyte*) generation. The elegant, arching, frond bearing plant that we instantly recognise and call a fern is the sporophyte or non-sexual stage. It is this plant's function to

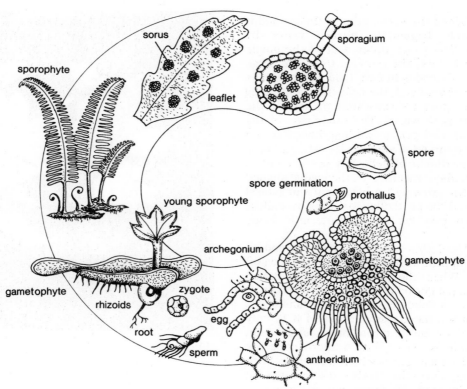

Fern life cycle

produce a minute spore which, when ripe, and if the surroundings are conducive to its growth, develops into a tiny plant called a *prothallus*. The prothallus is the fern's sexual stage and the one in which most of the action happens. It contains male and female components and, if there is sufficient moisture present, fertilisation of an egg cell takes place and the second generation plant or sporophyte grows, matures and bears spores.

That is the simple outline of the whole process. In detail it is intriguing, delicately balanced, finely tuned and engineered, highly complex and beautiful.

The single spore cell is the germ of life of another plant. It has little in common with the seed of a flowering plant, differing both in the nature of its construction and the principles of its growth. The spore commences its growth with the enlargement and multiplication of its single cell. Whichever part of this growing prothallus lies against the ground will form a root and whichever part faces upwards will form a structure that allows the plant to make food by photosynthesis. A seed, in comparison, is a miniature plant compressed into a tiny space. The embryo consists of two organs —a radicle, the germ of a future root, and a plumule, the germ of a future stem. Wherever or however the seed may fall there is no change in the respective functions of these two parts. The radicle will go down into the soil energy sources and the plumule will grow up to the light and air life sources.

The same conditions of growth must exist for the spore as for the mature fern, so if any one of the millions of spores released by the sporophyte falls upon a shady, moist place it will begin to grow. If at any stage of this initial growth conditions change for the worse the delicate thing will die. Its threads of existence are far more fragile than that of a seed for it has no reserves of food or moisture on which to draw.

When the spore falls to the ground it immediately begins to absorb water by osmosis. The tough outer wall of the single cell then bursts, the growing tissues emerge and the cell divides in two. One part becomes a root or *rhizoid* and, the cells now continuing to divide, grows downwards to anchor the plant and seek water. The other part of the original divided cell grows lengthways into a long green thread of single cells. After about a week this ribbon of cells has sent down its own rhizoids to maintain it, the wedge shaped cells at the growing tip have sent out lateral growth and the prothallus, as it is now called, begins to take on its characteristic heart shape.

Until this stage the growing spores will only appear as fine green scum on the soil surface. When the prothallus has finished developing, a period of about twelve weeks, it appears as a delicate and almost translucent heart shaped membrane. Most of it is only one cell thick and fine root hairs can be seen on its under-surface. With a microscope the male and female parts which have also been developing over the twelve weeks may be seen, and it is at this stage that all the action happens.

The female part, the *archegonium*, consists of a group of cells in a flask shape containing a single egg cell. When the egg is ripe the flask bursts open and secretes a malic acid which activates and attracts the spermatozoa that have formed in millions in the male cells, the *antheridia*. This is a surprising, almost animal-like action, and even more surprising, the spermatozoa are motile and actually swim to the egg cell.

The prothallus is an extraordinary plant in many ways; if fertilisation does not take place for some reason, usually lack of water, it may continue to live on for years. Moisture is essential as the antheridia can only open and release the spermatozoa when in contact with water and the spermatozoa can only move in water.

The spermatozoa are minute thread-like organisms with a bladder-like head and a coiled tail. The tail is covered with tiny hairs which rotate and propel the spermatozoa along in a spinning motion. This curious

A prothallus

motile sperm form of fertilisation takes place in all lower plants—mosses, horsetails and quillworts, for example—whose origins are still closely linked with the sea.

The spermatozoa are attracted to, and swim down the neck of the archegonium and, again animal-like, only one spermatozoon penetrates and fertilises the egg cell and growth of the fern as we recognise it begins — a grandchild as it were. The new plant is contained within and protected by the archegonium, drawing on the prothallus for food until it develops rhizoids of its own and the prothallus is withered and gone—its work done.

The first signs of growth of the sporophyte that are visible to the naked eye are embryonic fronds appearing from one part of the prothallus, and the classic crozier-like unfurling of the new growth of the true fern. The new fern gradually assumes the form and habit of the grandparent and when mature produces fertile fronds. On the back of these are produced, nursed and protected the tiny spores; and the whole life cycle begins again.

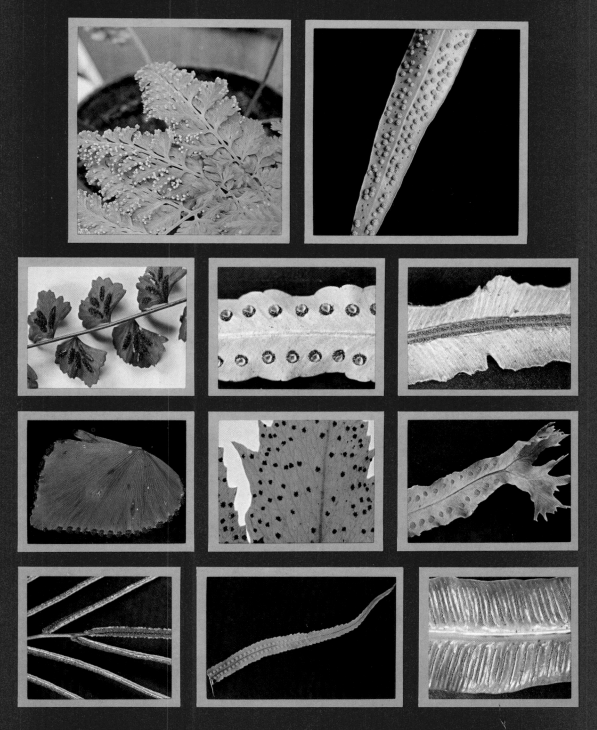

Different formations of sori found on the backs of fertile fronds

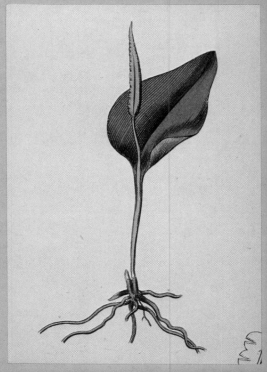

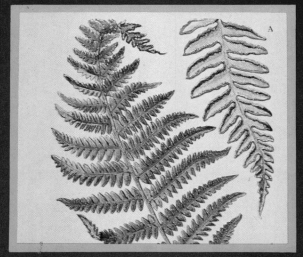

Top left: *Botrychium lunaria*, the mysterious moonwort of folklore
Top right: *Ophioglossum vulgatum*, a fern curiosity with historical
and mystical associations
Bottom: *Pteridium aquilinum*, once commonly called "Charles of the Oak"

OF FERNS AND MEN
2

F erns have had a long association with this earth. In comparison their period of popularity has been very brief. They have never been plants whose economic properties have been greatly valued by man and, until the middle of the nineteenth century, the Victorian era, they were not valued aesthetically.

Early collections

Before Victorian times there are records of a few fern collections in England dating from 1628 when John Tradescant, who owned a botanic garden and museum at Lambeth, in London, brought some rare plants back from a voyage to Virginia. Among the plants were two ferns — *Cystopteris bulbifera* and *Adiantum pedatum*. To this nucleus of a collection he added a *Camptosorus rhizophyllum* in 1680 and in 1699 an *Onoclea sensibilis*, both from America, and an *Adiantum reniforme* and a *Davallia canariensis* from Madeira. The only other recorded exotic fern in England at this time was a *Blechnum australe* in King Charles II's garden at Hampton Court. There is a record of this fern's being in the garden in 1671.

At the beginning of the eighteenth century there were only five species of exotic ferns in Britain. It was not until the 1770s that fern collecting began to gain popularity and be considered important botanically. Between 1770 and 1790 sixty-eight species were brought into Britain; most went into private collections and the rest into the official collection at Kew gardens.

The great Kew gardens at Richmond on Thames began as a small royal garden in 1759 as a hobby of George III's mother. It came under the patronage of Joseph Banks later in the century. Banks made great efforts to stimulate the introduction of new and rare plants by persuading commanders of ships of war and East Indiamen to take an interest in things botanical. In this way many plants were introduced to England, some of them living. A list of plants and general botanical guide was issued by the gardens in 1768. Under the grand title of *Hortus Kewensis*, this publication listed exotic plants including ten ferns. The second edition published in 1789 listed thirty-four ferns.

The collection was given a great boost in 1793 on the return of HMS *Providence* from its second voyage to the West Indian colonies. It was under the command of Rear Admiral Bligh who, whatever else was said of him, at least contributed greatly to botanical and scientific knowledge at the time. Thirty-seven ferns were among many plants that he brought back from this voyage.

The first ferns to arrive in England from Australia were brought back by George Caley in 1808. Originally a horse doctor from Birmingham, Cayley was sent to New South Wales by Joseph Banks to collect plants. Among those he collected were the ferns *Platycerium bifurcatum*, *Doodia aspera* and *Davallia pyxidata*. In 1816, another official collector, Alan Cunningham, sent several species from Australia and the first species from Norfolk Island. He was a veteran collector, having already spent several years with James Rowie in Brazil officially collecting for Kew gardens.

A dinner-table decoration from the Victorian era

Ferns displayed growing in the stem of a dead tree fern — Victorian ingenuity is displayed as well

John Smith and the Kew Collection

By the middle of the 1800s, exotic plants were arriving constantly at the Royal Botanic Gardens at Kew from new colonies and foreign places. Their arrival was always well publicised and attracted crowds of interested collectors and spectators. The Kew gardens had by this time quite an impressive collection of ferns under the tender care of John Smith who was curator there for forty years and a true fern fan. It was he who was responsible for the major acquisitions for the Kew fern collection.

At the beginning of the nineteenth century half the ferns at Kew were from the West Indies, four from the Cape of Good Hope, three from New Holland and one from St Helena. The rest were from North America and Madeira. But the collection was not in good hands and when John Smith took over as curator in 1822 he lamented that only forty species remained. What ferns were left were in very poor condition and the tropical species

almost non-existent. Smith found that the hothouses had been heated by brick flues which had not been well constructed. They leaked smoke and fumes and kept the atmosphere too dry and therefore unsuitable for good cultivation or even mere preservation of the ferns. So he set about putting them in order and organising the collection of new plants so effectively that Kew gardens became the botanical centre of Great Britain. By 1846 he was able to annouce proudly that there were 348 species in the fern houses.

Official collection was well under way with the patronage of the crown and wealthy scientifically minded gentlemen. Every opportunity was used to add to public and private collections. Contributions came from colonial botanical gardens and private individuals living in foreign countries.

The first species of *Grammitis billardieri* was sent to Kew in 1833 from the Sydney Royal Botanic Gardens, then under the direction of Richard Cunningham, and the then considered very curious *Platycerium superbum*, arrived at Kew from the botanic gardens in Brisbane a little later.

The first tree ferns caused a sensation when they arrived in 1841, sent by a New Zealand gardener Mr J. Edgerly. The two ferns, *Dicksonia squarrosa* and *Cyathea medullaris*, were greeted with delight and were immediately in great demand. In 1866 they were described in the British press as a great feature of an international exhibition in the Crystal Palace, "rearing their magnificent heads above the gorgeous collection of azaleas, roses etc.—indeed, but for the tree ferns, the exhibition would have lacked half its beauty and attraction as no other plants we have in cultivation would have substituted". Unfortunately these particular "majestic specimens" came to a premature end when fire destroyed the tropical end of the Crystal Palace.

Smith certainly did a great deal to promote the popularity of ferns with two books, endless official listings of new acquisitions and his general promotion of Kew as the botanical centre of Europe. He was very jealous of his fern charges and personally inspected a sizeable collection in

Berlin. He came back unimpressed and virtually inferred that the figures of the number of ferns in the collection were rigged!

He was kinder to local collectors and nurseries, however, encouraging, patronising, and conscientiously listing ferns in private collections and gardens. He maintained a friendly rivalry with other fern collectors and writers, as they did with him — it was after all a gentlemanly pursuit.

By 1857 Smith's *Catalogue of Cultivated Ferns* listed 560 exotic species in British gardens.

The Victorian Era

The Victorian era was the high point of popularity for ferns. They were considered a necessary decoration for the drawing rooms of the wealthy and humble alike and glasshouses and conservatories were built for their culture.

Tree ferns caused a sensation when introduced to Britain in 1841

A Victorian decoration featuring ferns and ivy

Their bright, graceful foliage offset the gloom and formality of the average Victorian home and their lavish, elaborate fronds appealed to the Victorians' passion for decorating everything in sight. They were grown in almost everyone's garden and graced almost everyone's parlour.

"No fête, horticultural exhibition, banquet or public dinner was successful without ferns to grace the occasion, for gay and brilliant colours alone will not satisfy the eyes of the horticultural public. Some happy change has come about in respect to floral exhibitions, also in the decoration of our gardens at home, both indoors and out — the rule being that flowering plants must have mixed with them a certain amount of ornamental foliage or the effect is not pleasing to the eye. Some, indeed, assert that a conservatory properly arranged with ornamental foliage plants and ferns alone, is the most effective." So wrote B. S. Williams, a well-known fern grower, collector and writer in his *Select Ferns and Cycopods* published in 1873. The Victorian fern craze was in full swing.

Elegant little conservatories of glass and lead were attached to parlours and sitting rooms. Here the house plants were rested after their indoor stay. If the family could not afford a conservatory, the precious fern collection was kept in a Wardian case; the then very fashionable and workable miniature glasshouse graced the parlour — along with the glass dome that covered waxed fruit and stuffed birds. In the conservatory or Wardian case the family collection was displayed prettily for interested admirers — and everyone was interested.

Botany was considered a most acceptable interest for any gentleman, and the collection and growing of ferns especially so. Commercial collectors and growers scoured the English countryside for the lovely indigenous species and hawked them from door to door in their baskets, along with the fishmongers and the muffinmen. So thorough was their collecting that many people believe the English countryside has never quite recovered from this vandalism. The *Adiantum capillus-veneris* and the *Asplenium ceterach* are now found in fewer numbers in their natural habitats in Great Britain because of this devastating collecting.

Anyone with time and/or money joined in the fashionable pursuit and ferns stayed in vogue for well over half a century. No other plant has been quite as popular for quite as long. During the eighteenth century tulips were fashionable. They were followed by the plants of the new world as they were rapidly discovered in that era of exploration. The heaths, proteas and aloes, and their kindred from New Holland and the Cape Colony were curiosities and were cherished and tended in homes and in the provincial botanical gardens being founded throughout England. These were followed in plant fashions by cacti from the new worlds. The more showy and easily cultivated of these unfriendly plants continued to be grown

A prized collection displayed in a hanging basket

through the first part of the 1800s but later John Smith, in one of his books about ferns, dismissed cacti as "scarcely saleable". But then he was a fern fancier! He also dismissed the more recently popular orchids as too difficult and too expensive to cultivate and as being "confined for the most part to the gardens of the wealthy". Ferns, he suggested, could be grown, as a general rule, in a comparatively inexpensive manner.

Gas heating and lighting meant the beginning of the end of ferns as indoor plants. Even though the Victorians understood their levels of tolerance of indoor atmospheres and dutifully whisked them in and out of ferneries and stove houses for rest and recuperation, the poisonous fumes and dry atmosphere created by the new-fangled heating appliances were too severe for the tender fern fronds and they were gradually replaced by tougher plants like palms and yuccas. Out of doors, though, in graceful little conservatories, contrived grottoes and miniature rockwork landscapes, ferns were still cultivated and much admired.

The turn of the century and the Edwardian era really brought an end to their popularity. Now everything had to be new, new, new and severely simple. Ferns were considered very *déjà vu* and far too evocative of the clutter and ornamentation of Victorian times to go with the new passion for clean lines and uncomplicated designs. The utterly simple palms and aspidistras were much more in keeping—ferns were too exuberant and luxurious for the new fad for elegance.

In a few years, the Great War of 1914-18 was almost to put an end to the growing of anything more exciting than a potato. Great areas of English public and private gardens, once devoted to growing beautiful and exotic plants for pleasure, were ploughed and turned over to vegetables to feed the people of the beleaguered country and the men who were defending it overseas. Many of those men were horticulturalists, collectors, botanists and just plain gardeners. Many of those men died in the mud and horror of it all and never came back to the gentle pastime of growing ferns and flowers for a living or just for pleasure. A lot of skill and a great many plants were lost forever and few nurseries and private gardens were to indulge in fern growing again on the scale of the Victorian era.

Wardian cases and glass fern shades

Nathaniel Bagshaw Ward, an eminent surgeon in London in the 1830s, invented the Wardian case. Actually, it was not really invented, it just happened.

Ward was a true Victorian gentleman, delving into all the sciences. Botany was one of his hobbies and ferns his special favourite. He had tried in vain to grow ferns and mosses on an old wall at his home in Finsbury Circus —a particularly smoggy part of London. He described the place as "surrounded by numerous manufactories and enveloped in their smoke", and was about to give up his fern ambitions in despair, when he was "led to reflect a little more deeply upon the subject in consequence of a simple incident which occurred in the summer of 1829". He recounted, "I had buried the chrysalis of a sphinx (moth) in some moist mould contained in a wide-mouthed glass bottle, covered with a lid. In watching the bottle from day to day, I observed that the moisture that during the heat of the day arose from the mould, became condensed on the internal surface of the glass, and returned whence it came, thus keeping the mould always in the same degree of humidity. Almost a week prior to the final changes of the insect, a seedling fern and a

grass made their appearance on the surface of the mould. I could not but be struck with the circumstance of one of that very tribe of plants, which I had for years fruitlessly attempted to cultivate, coming up *sponte sua* in such a situation; and asked myself seriously what were the conditions necessary for its growth. To this the answer was—firstly, an atmosphere free from soot; secondly, light; thirdly, heat; fourthly, moisture, and lastly, air." So Mr Ward's simple bottle was modified and elaborated on and became the functional, ornamental and fashionable Wardian case.

A Wardian fern case made by Eade & Son

Keen fern growers were able to cultivate a much wider range of species, especially those requiring warmth and a high degree of humidity in their atmosphere. The not-so-wealthy grower could afford a small case in which to display his collection and, above all, the cases were used by exploring botanists to send new and live plants back to the fascinated public who flocked to see the new arrivals at the Royal Botanic Gardens, Kew.

"It is a bit of the woodside sealed down with the life of the wood in it, and when unsealed for a moment it gives forth an odour that might delude us into the belief that we have been suddenly wafted to some dusky dell

The fern case was popular for species requiring extra humidity and protection

Glass domes were used to display tender ferns in carefully landscaped settings

where the nodding violet grows." This charming quote comes from a keen Victorian botanist, Shirley Hibberd, in one of his books *The Rambling Botanist*. He was an enthusiastic fern grower and wrote many books on the subject. In one of them he modestly but proudly claims that Mrs Hibberd's fernery has "nothing in England to surpass it in beauty and interest—though it is on an extremely small scale".

Hibberd experimented a great deal with growing ferns in sealed glass cases and had some very definite ideas on the art which he set forth categorically in his many books. He had some good ideas and some disasters too. He advises, in hindsight, to ensure that the glass dome type of case fits loosely into the pan which accompanies it. One of his shades "which was a tight fit was one day removed to a sunny window for a few hours to make room for some domestic operations. The sun heated the air within the shade, the expanded air had no means to escape, and it burst the shade with a loud explosion into a multitude of fragments. A guinea's worth of glass was thus lost in a moment and a collection of selaginellas placed in jeopardy through neglect of this precaution".

The simple glass dome was one of the many fern cases used in Victorian times. Glass had become a relatively cheap commodity, and the many inventors of the day constantly came up with bigger, better and brighter ideas for using it scientifically. The simplest form of fern shade was a bell glass and flower pot (invented by a Mr Fry and made by a Mr Pascall, a potter, of Chiselhurst). It consisted of a modified flower pot made of fine red terracotta ware, sometimes roughly ornamented, with a wide shallow rim around the top. A glass dome with a nice knob on top fitted into the rim which was then filled with water making the whole thing airtight. They were usually rather small, no more than forty centimetres (fifteen inches) high, and were considered a very neat table ornament.

Another form of the same kind of glass fern shade was a glass dish with a rim and a bell glass. The bigger versions of this were planted with elegant fern pillars (a Mr Rosher's patent idea). These were ornate fine porcelain pillars with holes around their sides. They were filled with damp compost and the holes planted with tiny ferns and fern allies. The plants were trimmed regularly so that the elegant support could still be seen and the whole topped with a miniature Grecian urn filled with a small cascading fern. Under the fragile glass dome the effect must have been lovely, but I doubt that many people bothered with the careful planting and tending required to keep the plants looking their best.

Larger, and more complicated, were the fern cases or Wardian cases constructed of wood and metal frames with boxes or troughs for the soil. They often had leg supports so that they were an independent piece of furniture and were often, too, fitted with castors so that they could be moved easily to make the most of daylight times in the house. While usually rectangular in shape and basically simple, in true Victorian style they became more and more elaborate and ornamented so that some fern growers had miniature Crystal Palaces in their sitting rooms.

Cases known as "Miss Maling's" were

Mr Rosher's elegant fern pillar was very lovely to look at but must have demanded very dedicated tending to keep it looking that way. The same sort of effect can be achieved today with rolled chicken wire filled with damp sphagnum moss

the most popular. They had simple rectangular outlines and could be heated, if required, by means of a gas flame or hot water, renewed periodically.

A patent case made by Gray of Danvers Street, Chelsea, had the optional extra of a boiler to afford warmth from below. The efficient boiler needed to be filled only once or twice a day in winter—fern growers would have to have been very dedicated in those days!

Inside the cases marvellous miniature landscapes and vistas were created with mountains, dells and streams. The recommended material for the rock work was common coke which added little in weight—relative to the weight of soil and moisture in the bigger cases. The secret of making the coke look like rock was to soak it in water and sprinkle it with a little Roman or Portland cement. This soon became coated with lichen and moss and looked just like aged rock.

But, beware, warned Mr Hibberd of "the niceties of gimcrackery—the grand thing is to have a sufficiency of healthy ferns of handsome varieties, everything else must be made subsidiary to that desideratum".

Economic uses

The more prosaic properties of most ferns are mucilaginous and slightly astringent fronds, bitter, astringent and rather acrid rhizomes and a very starchy make-up of their fleshier parts. Man has made use of these properties from time to time, but never in a big business way. One large, but short-lived business venture in the nineteenth century was the exporting of the beautiful, golden, silky hairs of a species of *Cibotium* common in the Sandwich Islands. The hairs were used to stuff pillows, but collapsed after a while and the trade, consequently, with them.

Ferns as Food

As a source of food ferns have mostly been used by the aboriginal inhabitants of a country. In New Zealand they were greatly valued by the Maoris for their edible parts. They baked the soft pith of the tree fern *Cyathea medullaris* to a reddish brown before eating it. The Maoris also used the large swollen scaly rhizomes of the *Marattia salicina* and the rhizomes of another New Zealand native, *Pteridium esculentum*, common bracken. These they roasted in ashes, peeled with their teeth and ate rather like bread. The Aborigines of New South Wales used to eat the rhizome of the bristle fern, *Blechnum cartilagineum*—said to taste rather like a waxy potato. It was roasted and then beaten to break down the woody fibre. In New Caledonia the soft pith at the base of the fronds of the tree fern, *Cyathea viellardi*, was extracted and eaten. The young shoots of king fern, *Angiopteris evecta*, of the Society Islands was eaten by the natives and a "flour" was made from its large rhizome. In the same islands the young fronds of the *Helminthostachys zeylanica* were prepared and eaten in the same way as asparagus.

Islanders of the Indian archipelago

used the succulent fronds of the curious water fern *Ceratopteris thalictroides* which were boiled and eaten as a vegetable. In the Fiji islands the young fronds of the balabala, *Alsophila lunulata*, are still eaten when other food is scarce. The original white settlers in these islands used the soft scales covering the stipes of the fronds of this plant to stuff pillows and cushions because they stayed much cooler than feathers on sultry tropical nights.

Of the European countries, Norway is the only one which has consistently used ferns as a food. There incipient fronds of the male fern, *Dryopteris filix-mas*, are plucked in their unfolded state and boiled and eaten as a kind of asparagus. This particular fern, along with the common bracken, has been used in times past throughout northern Europe in brewing ale and evidently imparts a special flavour to it. Proportions used in the manufacture are one part of the rhizome to two parts of malt. A less potent beverage — tea — was made from the fronds of *Dryopteris fragrans*.

These days for tastes that lean to the exotic in food, there are the fiddleheads of ferns, like the *Matteuccia struthiopteris*, or better still the "Fiddlehead Ferns Gratinées", a specialty of the spring menu at the Four Seasons Restaurant in New York. The recipe is published in the *Four Seasons Cookbook* by Charlotte Adams, who describes them as a vegetable "unique in flavour and delightful in appearance". The recipe directs blanching 1 kg (2 lb) of fiddlehead ferns in 1.5 L (3 qt) of boiling water for five minutes, draining them well then tossing them in browned clarified butter for three minutes. For the gratinée, they are mixed with a béchamel sauce, sprinkled with cheese and browned under a grill.

Medicinal Uses

Over the centuries ferns have probably been used most widely and frequently for medicinal purposes. Like many ancient remedies and medicines some involving ferns are very fanciful, such as the seventeenth century herbalist Culpepper's advice to burn the male fern and use the smoke to drive away "serpents, gnats and other noisome creatures which in ferny countries do in the night time trouble and molest people lying in their beds with their faces uncovered". In very ancient times the Greek botanist Dioscorides recommended the same fern "against the stinging and biting of serpents".

An old wives' remedy that was used until the turn of this century was a healing ointment called "Adder's Spear Ointment" made from the adder's tongue fern, *Ophioglossum vulgatum*. It was made of the leaves infused or boiled in oil of unripe olives and set in the sun for a number of days. This "herb" according to Culpepper was under the dominion of the moon and Cancer and owed its name to a reputed power to cure the bites of adders and other reptiles.

Serpents, adders and sundry reptiles we can cope with by other means these days, but there are some fern remedies that are quite plausible and seem to have stood the test of time. They have been a most effective cure for intestinal worms. Both the male fern and the common bracken are powerfully astringent medicines and have been used since the days of Dioscorides as a vermifuge. The vermifuge is made from the dried root stock powder mixed with honey or syrup and administered as an electuary.

Ferns have been used widely, too, for the treatment of liver and allied complaints. "Spleenworts", a name used formerly for the Aspleniums, were so called because of their frequent use in the treatment of liverish complaints and "swelling of the spleen". *Asplenium ruta-muraria*, wall rue, once had the curious name of "tentwort" and was used widely to cure rickets, a disease formerly called the "taint". At the beginning of this century in parts of Cumberland County in England, the royal fern, *Osmunda regalis*, was a popular remedy for this disease.

The spleenworts had many other uses too. The common maidenhair spleenwort, *Asplenium trichomanes*, was once used in the Scottish highlands as a form of tea for coughs and colds, and about three centuries ago a herbalist recommended it to stop hair falling out. Ideal if you were a balding consumptive.

The sea spleenwort, *Asplenium marinum* was used hundreds of years ago for the relief of burns, and the scaly spleenwort, *Asplenium ceterach*, was used as a bait for rock cod on some parts of the Welsh coast. If the fishing was not good, you could be cheered by boiling and eating the roots of the same fern as it was considered a remedy for "all melancholy"—a recommendation of Culpepper's.

The polypody, *Polypodium vulgare*, was once used as a purgative and a cure-all for chest complaints including whooping cough. The dried rhizomes were crushed and taken mixed with honey. Culpepper ascribes some remarkable qualities to the three-branched polypody or "Polypody of the Oak" as he calls it. (This is most probably the oakfern, *Gymnocarpium dryopteris*, formerly known as *Polypodium dryopteris*.) It was supposedly very good for those troubled with melancholy or "Quartan Agues". He suggested that the remedy be taken in honeyed water, barley water or the broth of a chicken together with beets and mallows. The same concoction was ordered for "fearful and troublesome sleeps and dreams".

There is a story of an ointment made from the fern *Stachys palustris*, commonly called clown's woundwort, used by village women in Buckinghamshire. The herbalist Gerard, who gave the plant its English name, said that he did so because of the "clownish answer" which he received from "a very poore man" who had cut his leg to the bone and healed it with this plant. Gerard tells us that he "offered to heale the same for charitie, which he refused, saying that I coulde not heale it so well as himselfe".

The rootstock of the royal fern, *Osmunda regalis*, was also reputed to possess the quality of healing wounds, whether applied to them externally or taken internally in the form of a decoction. Its outward application was considered effective for bruises, sprains and broken bones.

In more recent years the British native maidenhair, *Adiantum capillus-veneris*, was used as the principal ingredient for a popular French pectoral remedy called "Capillaire". It was made by adding to 30 g (1 oz) of the fronds of the maidenhair 7.5 g (¼ oz) of liquorice root and 0.5 L (1 pt) of boiling water. The ingredients were steeped for six or seven hours and strained. To this was added 0.14 L (¼ pt) of orange flower water and 1 kg (2 lb) of loaf sugar. The North American maidenhair, *Adiantum pedatum*, having the same properties, could be used as a substitute. The wall rue, *Asplenium ruta-muraria* and the black spleenwort, *Asplenium adiantum-nigrum*, were considered to have the same properties to a lesser degree.

In recent years, too, ferns have been used widely as drugs and ointments for more specific purposes. In Peru the rhizomes of the two polypodies, *Polypodium angustifolium* and *P. crassifolium*, are used with those of the *Elaphoglossum huacsaro* as diaphoretics to induce perspiration and as astringents. The same drug was supposed to have fever reducing and anti-rheumatic properties. This medication was quite well known in Europe early this century.

In northern Asia the disease scurvy was treated with a medication made from the fronds of the *Dryopteris fragrans*. Ferns also appear in Oriental medicine. The herbarium of the British Museum has specimens of the densely clothed rhizomes of a species of *Davallia* used in Chinese medical practice. And in India *Notholaena piloselloides* was used to subdue sponginess of the gums.

The marvellously exotic sounding Penghawar-djambi—a drug sold in Europe in the nineteenth century—was made in Java from the lovely, sparkling, golden hairs on the lower stems of *Dicksonia* and *Cibotium* species and used as a styptic—a check for external and internal bleeding. It is listed in a German pharmacopoeia of the time.

Miscellaneous Uses

The astringent qualities of some fern parts have been made use of in dressings for leather and in the manufacture of soap. In northern Britain the roots of the British native brake, *Pteridium aquilinum*, were collected, dried in the sun and made into little balls of soap for washing clothes. The native brake was used frequently too for thatching houses, but probably most Britons would remember it being used as a lining for strawberry punnets in early summer. It was packed around fresh fruit and fish because of its resistance to mildew and an ability to impart to and retain freshness in foodstuffs.

Farmers have used bracken for fattening pigs as, like the male fern, it contains a great deal of starch. For a food for pigs the young shoots were simmered in water for several hours and the resulting jelly fed to the animals. In Norway, the incipient fronds of the male fern are gathered in the summer, dried, and when winter comes given to the cattle after being soaked in water to reconstitute them. On the farm too the ashes of the male fern have been used as a valuable nitrogenous fertiliser, especially valuable in growing potatoes.

Today the practical use of ferns is very limited. The culinary delights of the fiddleheads of ferns have been mentioned. There remains only the use of ferns to make a natural dye. In her book, *Weaving, Spinning and Dyeing*, Virginia G. Hower gives a recipe for using the tender young fronds of any fern to make a delightful stable, light yellowish-green dye. The dye is made from 500 g (1 lb) of young fronds or 1 kg (2 lb) of mature fronds, first simmered in water for two hours then strained. To the pulp is added enough water to make the mix up to 20 L (4 gal). The material to be dyed is rinsed and fixed in alum or chrome before immersion in the dyepot, brought gradually to the boil and simmered for one hour. Once cool, the cloth is rinsed several times in water of decreasing temperatures then dried. A cup of household ammonia added to the dyebath gives a brighter colour.

Scythian lamb. Travellers to central Europe and Asia in the 1700s brought back strange stories of a charm in the shape of a lamb. It was fashioned from the caudex of the plant *Dicksonia barometz* and was hung in the house of the superstitious to ward off evil. The long silky hairs when dried resembled wool and a small piece with the stalks of the fronds still attached *did* look like a lamb

Folklore

The powers to impart invisibility, unshoe a horse, unlock doors, fend off the devil and his minions and change quick silver into real silver, have all been accredited to the fern in times past. It has been acclaimed as the essential ingredient in a love potion and said to carry the mark of the devil. Innocent or otherwise, it has been the source of folklore and mysticism as well as an inspiration for poets and painters right up to the late nineteenth century.

The curious little moonwort, *Botrychium lunaria*, has a long association with fairies and things magical. It is an unusual fern which, to quote a nineteenth century fern admirer, "grows apart from its kind, on the open face of meadows, under the play of moonbeams". It was treated with great respect in medieval times as it was thought to have the power to open locks and unshoe horses that trod in the meadows where the plant grew. It earned the names "blasting roots" and "spring wurzel" for such amazing feats. Country people avoided and feared it for its supposed powers over metal, while at the same time alchemists prized it for its supposed powers to change quicksilver into real silver.

The fairies were thought to have used the moonwort to saddle their horses and indeed the leaflets do look just like a saddle where they spread themselves out and away from the stem. Shakespeare tells us that Queen Mab saddled her steed with the pinnules of the moonwort and galloped "night by night through lovers' brains, and then they dream of love".

If Queen Mab and her magical moonwort failed to stir good feelings perhaps a potion mixed from the male fern, *Dryopteris filix-mas*, worked better. It was an essential and prize ingredient in a love potion and if it was mixed by a witch, chances were that it would be even more successful. If it was successful in love only those who took it knew, but put to broader use it was considered a very favourable good luck charm if the rhizome was dried in the smoke of a midsummer fire and fashioned into the shape of the fingers of a hand. I am not sure if this fact should be spread around, but the same magical powers were attributed to the lady fern, *Athyrium filix-femina*, though they were thought to be not as powerful.

The fern features in the all powerful *Doctrine of Signature*. This was the creed relating to the interpretation of shapes and patterns formed when connecting bundles of tissues in roots, stems and leaves of plants are cut horizontally and it greatly influenced the simple and superstitious of olden days. The pattern found in the tissues of the bracken *Pteridium aquilinum* formed the

letter "C" and was taken to be Christ's initial so the fern was prized as a protection against witches and goblins and other emissaries of the devil. In Scotland the letter "X" was found in the tissues of the same fern. This, being the ancient Greek symbol for Christ, was another good sign. However, there is also a record of the mark of the devil's hoof in the tissues of the roots of a bracken found in Scotland, so it seems that this fern had a rather chequered career in the north of Britain. In parts of England the bracken has also been called "King Charles in the Oak Tree" because the picture depicted in the stem fibres is that of the King hiding in a tree to escape his enemies.

The mysterious way in which a fern reproduced itself caused wonder and speculation for centuries, and in their ignorance people thought that the "invisible" seed had the power to impart the same potential to its finder. Shakespeare refers to it in *Henry IV* when Chamberlain says to Gadshill "You are more beholding to the night than to fern seed for your walking invisible".

Many pagan ceremonies sprang up around this belief in the fern's power to render invisible the finder of its seed. One of them was to "catch" the fern seed. Twelve pewter plates were taken at midnight of St John's Eve and placed under the "black spotted frond" (it was thought that the black spots had something to do with seeding and fell suddenly on Midsummer Eve). The magical seed in falling would pass through eleven of the plates and rest on the twelfth. Fairies, however, were sometimes there too to snatch the seed away as it fell. If the gatherer succeeded in his attempt to "catch" the seed on the twelfth plate he would thereafter possess the much coveted quality of invisibility. As late as the nineteenth century this superstition still existed in Britain amongst country people in Worcestershire.

CULTIVATION
3

The way to grow ferns is to understand them, and a close look at the places in which they grow naturally will help. Though ferns grow in all climatic zones from temperate to tropical their natural habitat is moist, sun-sheltered by tall trees, protected from wind and often on the sides of mountains away from the sea, where moisture-laden clouds first drop gentle rain.

Let's have a closer look at one of the places where ferns naturally flourish — a gully on the side of a mountain where a stream constantly trickles.

High overhead will be a great canopy of trees and, under that, a spread of lovely arching tree ferns. The trunks of the trees on the side closest to the mountain will be enveloped in aerial ferns, and tiny crevices in the rocky walls of the gully will hold bouquets of cascading fronds. Climbing ferns will have found their way to the low growing branches of the great trees, and, from there, they will have spread out, and along to smaller trees, covering the younger and softer ones with a massive mantle of green.

On the ground in this lush place there will be the terrestrial ferns, binding together the mass of moulding leaves and twigs that clothe the forest floor. Under those spreading ground ferns, are the tiny new sporophytes and mosses, and closer to the damp earth again, the green film of the developing prothalli.

The light is dappled, filtering softly through the overhead trees. The air is still, winds and draughts broken down to gentle eddies by the mountain boulders and massive trunks of ancient trees. The atmosphere is cool and moist, with vapours from the damp floor and oozing rocks trapped within the gully's confines by the trees and rocks. Sometimes the moisture in the air is so heavy that it condenses on the overhead fronds and drops gently back to the soft earth below. This earth is a matted mass of fallen leaves, fronds, twigs and bark and, under that, a denser mat of half-rotted matter, barely recognisable as the leaves and twigs that once they were. And under that, it is a dark brown sticky mass that is almost one with the earth below.

Water is in this layer, too, sometimes enough to squelch beneath the feet — water that is fresh and clear and moving; constantly trickling away and being replenished by tiny rivulets that spread down and through the rocks and soil. For ferns love water — cool, fresh, misty raindrops on their fronds and soft, fresh water about their roots.

None of these conditions is impossible to recreate. They can be easily and ingeniously reproduced in glasshouses, shade houses, in the open garden and in the house without too much expense or trouble. All that is needed, basically, is an awareness of ferns' natural state and the wherewithal (and that does not necessarily mean money!) to recreate it for them.

Light requirements

All plants need natural light to manufacture food by the process called "photosynthesis". Light rays, chiefly the red, blue and violet, are the energy sources that plants use to fuse water and carbon dioxide within the leaf to form the plant's food, sugar. Some plants can carry out this process in a wide range of light conditions. Ferns, on the whole, prefer degrees of shade for this process.

At both ends of this shade scale ferns will probably grow, usually struggling on for a while, for they are adaptable, until the harsh reality of the situation gets the better of them, and they succumb and die — slowly and horribly, for they are both hardy and sensitive. Too strong a light, or full sunshine for a significant part of the day, can alter the appearance of a fern. Fronds and stems become thicker, the fronds become smaller, less luxuriant, and quite yellow. It looks tougher than a fern grown in softer light. A fern will adapt to such a situation by altering its appearance, but, if the sunlight becomes too hot and a harsh drying wind reaches even those tough fronds, and if the roots dry out on such a day, the plant could wilt and die, or at the least be severely set back.

Light intensified through a pane of glass can "fade" a fern. This often happens with a plant kept by a window inside a house. If it is kept too close to a window that gets direct and strong light for a greater part of the day, the fronds will take on a greyish, translucent quality which makes the whole plant look old and very fragile.

Too little light will make a fern react in much the same way as any plant that is deprived of sufficient light for its needs. The fronds become elongated and spindly. Because the plant has little in the way of stored energy to call on, the production of new fronds falls off and existing growth, which cannot manufacture food, yellows and drops off. Without fronds, old and new, growth slows down, eventually ceases and, of course, the plant dies.

The older the plant, the more light it requires. The prothallus grows low down on the soil, shaded and protected by the fronds of the parent plant, but needs more light as the true fern develops and the fronds grow in size and become more complicated in structure. So, when introducing a baby plant to a collection it will grow best if well sheltered under a bigger plant until it is of comparable size. Ferns growing in adequate light have large and luxuriant fronds and are better able to cope with other stresses that are put on them by container growing and other contrived conditions.

By observing the colour and general look of ferns it is possible to see at a glance if the fronds are looking dull or pale through too much light or if they have been in the dark for too long and are looking a bit stretched out and limp. Their reactions to light intensities are not immediate. A day or two will tell if the light is too strong, and within a week or two, there will be evidence of insufficient light. You should, though, act immediately if you suspect that light intensities are not correct. Ferns are hardy and do recover from little setbacks, but it is asking much of them to let them get to a point where they are being constantly set back or are only just "getting by".

Though all ferns become more demanding when grown indoors, the needs of individual ferns will vary of course. For example, one may tolerate only a few days near a certain window before it looks a little wan and may need four or five days outside to pick up. Another may tolerate that same situation

much longer. The changing intensity and angle of light through the changing seasons will also affect plants grown indoors and it may take a fair amount of juggling of spaces and plants, and organising blinds and reflectors, to keep indoor ferns happy in the same space all the year round.

Atmosphere

A moist atmosphere is essential to ferns' well being. They need at least 30 per cent, but do better at 60-80 per cent relative humidity during the day, and a slightly lower reading at night. This applies to ferns in the house, glasshouse, and shade house and is the key to successful growing of ferns as indoor plants.

Low humidity seems to inhibit new growth, causing it to shrivel. Old established growth yellows or the edges of the leaflets go brown and the whole frond becomes brittle, eventually dropping off in protest. Conversely, an excessively high humidity is not necessarily better for ferns. The lower night time humidity is necessary—not only because it duplicates natural outdoor conditions but it also inhibits the growth of moulds.

The various methods of increasing the moisture content of the air are discussed in detail in the chapters to do with keeping plants in the house (page 54), glasshouse (page 53), and shade house (page 52).

Air

If the air in a room which contains plants seems fresher, it *is* possibly fresher, because plants take up carbon dioxide from the atmosphere (the waste gas that animals exhale from their lungs) and use it in their energy making process, photosynthesis. Photosynthesis results in the release of oxygen into the air. A little carbon dioxide is released in the respiration process during the hours of darkness, when photosynthesis actually stops. The very small amount of stale gas does not warrant the removal of plants from a room at night, as was so assiduously done in bygone days.

This need for carbon dioxide does not mean that a fern, or any plant for that matter, will thrive in a "stale" atmosphere. They need oxygen for respiration the same as any living thing. Respiration is carried out in the same cells as is photosynthesis but, unlike photosynthesis which is a daytime activity only, respiration is a continuing process.

So ferns *must* have fresh air. Smog, fumes from gas, oil smoke, rooms constantly filled and warmed with body heat (such as restaurants) are devastating for them over long periods and certainly damaging over short ones.

Flinging open a window and letting in a sudden change of air will not always be beneficial. You may feel instant relief, but a plant's metabolism is much slower and adjustments are made gradually. So, a blast of cold air may be just as devastating as the "fug" which a plant has to tolerate. A gradual change to a cooler airy situation is what is needed. Constant draughts, hot or cold, even sneaky little ones from under a closed window, will damage delicate fern fronds. New growth will remain stunted on the side that is exposed to the draught. This is a source of damage to be checked if plants are looking lopsided.

A constant but gentle flow of fresh moist air is what is most beneficial to ferns growing in an enclosed atmosphere, such as indoors or in a glasshouse. Gentle little eddies should continually move around and among the fronds, constantly replenishing the life giving air and moving used gases and dangerous fungus spores.

Soil

Soil pH

Generally ferns prefer an acid soil and grow best at a pH of between 6 and 7, and the majority will not grow in any but acid conditions. Simple soil testing kits can be bought from nurseries, or if the whole garden is to be tested, the local Department of Agriculture usually provides a service for a small fee.

In their natural state ferns take root in the spongy layer of leaf mould and humus that has accumulated on the forest floor for centuries. This decayed matter is rich in nitrogen and on the acid side of the pH scale.

This does not mean, however, that you should immediately take steps to increase the acidity of the soil in which ferns are growing. If they are growing well, leave the soil alone. If they are not growing well, check first for other adverse conditions before assuming that the soil is not sufficiently acid.

It does not mean, either, that all ferns hate lime, for there are many including the spleenworts and the hartstongues which are native to areas of limestone and grow happily among calcium containing rocks. And many ferns, for example the parsley fern *Cryptogramma crispa*, prefer an acid soil but will get by in fairly neutral territory.

It is much more difficult to increase the acidity of an alkaline soil than it is to increase the alkalinity of an acid soil. It can be done with the application of sulphur, and with the continual application of leaf mould. However, applying sulphur is a tricky business and should be done after a soil test by the Department of Agriculture and on its recommendation.

If the soil is too acid, it can usually be altered by adding lime. But lime increases the alkalinity, so it is not practicable in a fern bed. In this case, gypsum (calcium sulphate) can be added for though it does not reduce the soil acidity it is especially useful in the fern bed for reducing stickiness in clay soils and as a general soil conditioner. Rates of application depend on soil types. Clay soil needs two and a half times as much gypsum to correct the same degree of acidity as would a sandy soil, so it is best to test soil first.

Soil Texture

The soil texture, too, is important to successful fern growing. Ferns' roots are delicate, fibrous and shallow, designed to cling to soft layers of decayed vegetation. Their roots are not strong and searching like a tree's, which must anchor itself against the elements and constantly search new territory for food. Ferns get all sustenance that they need from the rich organic matter close at hand and, in the sheltered places in which they grow, do not need to batten down against the wind.

The soil for successful fern growing should be soft and fibrous so that it is moisture retentive, coarse and fairly open so that it will drain readily, and slightly on the acid side of the pH scale.

The structure of the soil can be changed for the better, or "conditioned" by using soil additives, organic or inorganic. A soft fibrous texture can be obtained by adding organic matter to the soil in the garden, or to the ingredients of a potting mixture in the form of the following: leaf mould (partly decayed leaves), well decayed garden compost (made without lime), peat moss, wood shavings, sawdust, finely shredded bark, buzzer chips, tree fern fibre (this is the coarse dust and particles that result from a chain saw being used on tree fern trunks), very old manure, spent hops and rice husks. Inorganic substances such as perlite (material derived from the expansion of siliceous rock), styrofoam beads, and vermiculite will also do the job of keeping a soil mixture in the garden or in a pot soft. Coarse sand (quartz sand and builders' sand which must be washed to prevent it from setting hard), gravel, scoria, crushed rock, charcoal pieces (which also assist in keeping the soil "sweet" by their ability to absorb impurities in the soil) are all inorganic and assist in keeping the growing medium open, aerated and draining effectively.

In the garden the structure can be altered for fern growing by the addition of any one, some or all of the substances just mentioned. A closer look at each will explain how it affects the ground.

Leaf mould: This organic matter formed by partially decayed leaves is excellent humus forming material and one of the finest soil conditioners for ferns. The best type of leaf mould is considered to be that from oak and beech leaves. When these delicate deciduous leaves are in the process of breaking down, they are rich in many nutrients and have a strong fibrous texture and a crumbly consistency. Other deciduous tree leaves are not as good as oak and beech for this purpose, but they are better than nothing.

Leaf mould can, of course, be gathered from the bush and fern gullies, but this is illegal in many parts of the world. What little bush we have left is too precious to abuse.

Leaf mould can be made from autumn's fallout by building a frame (it can be an elaborate structure made from wood and wire, or a simple one of criss-crossed light branches and twigs) and on this piling all the autumn leaves layered with a few spadefuls of earth. If placed in shallow heaps of not more than 1 m high, a lovely fibrous mould will result after about a year. This makes an ideal compost for the fern bed, and solves the problem of what to do with the masses of leaves that a big garden can produce, and which can overwhelm the normal compost heap. Standard compost can then be made with the addition of lime for the rest of the garden.

Compost: Made from well-decayed garden and kitchen waste, compost can go into fern bed soil, but should be avoided if a lot of lime has been added to it to assist its decomposition. A satisfactory compost can also be made from coarse garden waste, such as light prunings, and tough, stalked plants like dahlias which take a long time to break down in the compost heap. They can be heaped in an out-of-the-way corner of the garden and there left to take their own, longer time to break down. The resulting compost is tough, fibrous matter which makes a good conditioner for heavy soil.

Peat moss: This is the ideal organic matter for fern soils as it provides resilience, aeration and water retentive properties for the soil. It is partly or wholly decomposed moss or mosses such as sphagnum moss. It is sun or kiln dried, and then shredded into various grades.

Peat moss actually contains about twice as much nitrogen as do manures but it is not in a form that is available to plants, and therefore should be regarded as a soil conditioner, not as a fertiliser. In a pot or in the ground, it breaks down slowly, keeping the soil loose over a long period of time, and improving the aeration and drainage for that time.

There are various qualities of peat. Avoid the very black type which feels greasy and becomes sticky and adhesive when wet. For ferns, sedge peat should be avoided too, because it does not contain moss and may contain salts. Fine, dusty peat is useless. The best quality peat is brown and spongy or fibrous, or black and fluffy. Both these types are relatively light.

Sometimes peat moss is sold in such a dehydrated form that it is very difficult to handle. It can be better managed by adding water (warm water acts more quickly) through a small opening in the bag, and leaving it to soak through the fibres. This can sometimes take a day or two if the bag is big and the peat moss very dry. This soil conditioner should be evenly moist before you use it. Never mix dry peat moss into a potting mixture. It will be almost impossible to mix evenly, and more importantly, it will take up the moisture from the other ingredients and in the absorption process swell up and dislodge otherwise firmly potted plants.

Peat moss is expensive and becoming more and more difficult to obtain, so despite its long lasting qualities, it is not an economical proposition to add to a fern bed. Perhaps it's a little luxury best kept for potted plants.

Wood products: Sawdust, wood chips, buzzer chips, pine bark and wood shavings and other wood waste products contribute greatly to the structure of the soil, but add very little in the way of nutrients. They can actually, in their breaking down process, rob the soil of some of its nitrogen, because the micro-organisms which convert the wood particles to humus need mineral nutrients to grow. You should bear this in mind and use these products with care, and add fertiliser to the soil on a regular basis during their decomposition.

Sawdust is best used after it has been allowed to decompose for about twelve months, with a little animal manure added to speed the process.

Lately pine bark has come to be considered the likely substitute for peat moss, and an important ingredient in potting mixtures. It comes in various grades. A fine grade with particles of less than 6 mm (¼ in), with at least 40 per cent of a size greater than 1 mm (1/16 in) is ideal for potting mixtures. A coarser grade can be used in the garden and as drainage material in big pots. Pine bark has the same disadvantage as other wood products in that it fixes nitrogen in the soil, but an advantage in that bark breaks down more slowly than wood, so the life of the soil conditioner lasts longer.

Tree fern fibre: Tree fern fibre, which is the fine, dark, sweet smelling material resulting from the use of a chain saw on the trunks of tree ferns, makes an ideal soil conditioner for ferns. Like other wood products, it is not decomposed and is best left to break down for twelve months. The resulting humus is used as a soil conditioner. It has the advantage of containing a range of fibres, from the dense particles of the centre wood to the fine strands and soft tissues which make up the outer layers of the trunk.

It is difficult to get, and I can only suggest that you watch for a nurseryman who carries a range of containers made of tree fern wood, and ask him to order a bag of tree fern fibre from his supplier. Do make sure that your nurseryman's supplier is a reputable fellow—it would be awful to support someone indirectly who is illegally taking these trees from the bush. If osmunda fibre is available use it as a soil conditioner. It has a stronger texture than does tree fern fibre and thus allows maximum root penetration.

Seaweed: Seaweed has become a fashionable soil conditioner since people have realised how cheap and effective it is as mulch in times of drought. The mulch, once broken down to humus, makes an excellent soil conditioner. It is rich in nitrogen in a readily available form, providing nearly as much nitrogen and up to three times as much potash as an equivalent dressing of cow manure. However, it must be very thoroughly washed before using on a fern bed, and do not rely on it for too many years as it will gradually increase the alkalinity of the soil. Though it should be used with caution, it is

Top: *Nephrolepis exaltata* var. *bostoniensis* cv. Golden Boston and
Davallia fejeensis cv. Minor
Bottom left: *Azolla pinnata* covers the surface of a small pool
Bottom right: *Asplenium nidus* and *Platycerium superbum* in rainforest habitat

Top: *Nephrolepis cordifolia* lends its softening effect to an entrance way
Bottom left: Overhead lattice filters the light in this ideal
sheltered position for ferns
Bottom right: *Asplenium nidus* and *Platycerium superbum*

A cool sunroom makes an ideal setting for *Lygodium japonicum* in the
hanging brass pot, *Microlepia strigosa* to the left in the foreground
and *Nephrolepis biserrata* cv. Furcans

Top: Ferns are at home in this period Victorian interior
Bottom: Two tree ferns unfurling their fronds.
The setting, the light and the space are all ideal for them

probably the cheapest and most readily available of the soil conditioners.

Manure: Manure should be used more for its humus qualities as a top dressing in a fern garden or as a top-up for a plant that has been in its pot for a long time. It is essential that it is old and thoroughly decomposed as it can generate a great deal of heat as it breaks down and will burn roots and trunks it comes into contact with.

Avoid using it, no matter how old it is, in conditions where the humidity is very high, as it encourages the growth of bacteria and mould.

Hops and other cereals: Spent hops can sometimes be obtained from breweries, and are useful for improving the physical condition of the soil, but are very low in nutrients. The same is true of rice and oat husks.

Sand: I am sure that every recipe for potting mixture ever written has suggested using coarse river sand to make up at least one-third of the components. Any grade of sand is added to soils to increase the aeration and drainage, in the garden and in a pot.

If a heavy loam is added to a potting mixture, a coarse grade of sand is recommended; if the loam is already very sandy, the sand can be omitted altogether. Unwashed builder's sand sets and goes very hard after it has been wetted and worked so it is best to avoid it. The same goes for sand from the beach, unless washed very thoroughly. Then it is still suspect as it contains shell grit which has a very high salt content.

Vermiculite: This is a mineral, mica, which has been heated at great temperature until it expands like popcorn, and becomes a sponge which can absorb eight times its weight of water. The intense heat used in its preparation leaves it quite sterile. Its sponge-like quality makes it ideal as a water retentive material, and it contains a little potassium and calcium in a form available to plants. Its surface provides a favourable site for the movements of minerals within the soil mix. Vermiculite is not a long term soil conditioner as it tends to break down easily.

Perlite: Perlite does not collapse as easily as vermiculite. It is a sterile, inorganic material which comes from vitreous rock broken up by minute spherical cracks, again providing aeration for soil and soil mixes.

Scoria: This is being used more and more in potting mixes and is quite suited as a medium for growing ferns. On its own it will not grow plants, but mixed with nutrients makes a good substitute for soil and sand. Because of its high pH value, nutritional problems such as iron deficiency may develop with prolonged use.

Brown coal: In Australia, brown coal has recently been shown by the Victorian Department of Agriculture's research station at Knoxfield to be useful as a soil additive when combined with other materials, or as a substitute for soil on its own. Its main disadvantage is that it does not form a good mixture with soil because it tends to waterlog easily. On the other hand, it mixes and binds well with other materials.

Suggested mixtures are one part by volume of brown coal with one part of coarse sand or scoria; or one part of brown coal with one part of pine bark or peat moss. It has a pH of from 6.0 to 6.5, which is ideal for ferns. Some sort of follow-up fertiliser is recommended by the Department.

Charcoal: A form of carbon, charcoal is a black porous substance made by partly burning wood, bones and animal or vegetable waste. Mixed through soil, it acts as a filter, constantly absorbing toxic materials that accumulate through watering. If waterlogging is suspected in the ground or in a pot, charcoal will counteract this to a marked extent.

Watering

Ferns should be watered when they need it, and must never be allowed to wilt. There are no rules, no time schedules. Nothing precise like numbers of days or weeks and no details like amounts of water per cubic centimetre of soil. It has nothing to do with the time of the year, the phases of the moon, or the state of the gardener's corns.

There are a few guidelines and many factors to consider. The soil around the roots of most ferns, in the ground or in a pot, must be kept moist; and there is a great deal of difference between "wet" and "moist". "Moist" is an even dampness throughout the soil. "Wet" is a state of constant sogginess that excludes oxygen from the soil bacteria and the roots of the plant. In this state the bacteria die and the whole lot becomes a sour smelling, slimy mess. Another point: ferns like more water than most other house plants growing under similar conditions.

You must take into consideration the weather—the temperature and atmospheric conditions if ferns are growing under cover, or in a house, and the season and its influence on growth patterns. Plants will need less watering during cool weather when evaporation from the soil and moisture loss through the leaves is less; and more frequent watering when the warmer weather, with its usually drier atmosphere, extracts moisture from the soil and the fronds transpire more.

The size and make-up of a container in which a plant is growing also affect watering requirements. A plant in a small pot will be growing at the same rate as one in a big pot, if they are growing under the same conditions, so, of course, will use just as much water. So a small potted plant will have to be watered more often than a big one. A plant growing in a plastic or glazed pot will not need as much watering as one growing in an unglazed earthenware container, because a considerable amount of moisture is lost through the sides of a clay pot. But then, a clay pot will actually hold more moisture than a plastic pot of the same size because it retains moisture within its walls, and will, therefore, keep the soil cooler on a hot day. (The pros and cons of plastic and clay pots are discussed in the chapter on container growing, on page 60.)

The kind of potting mixture in which a plant is growing must be taken into consideration too. A heavy loam and dense peat or leaf mould combination will retain moisture much longer than an open mix of big fibre particles and coarse sand. But a mix that is too heavy and moisture retentive is prone to wetness if carelessly watered, and that brings many problems.

When to Water

There are several ways, scientific and unscientific, of telling if a plant should be watered. Some of the unscientific methods seem downright emotional.

Once a routine of caring for plants has been established, watering will become second nature, and something that is entirely between you and your charges. I find I am defending more and more an instinctive feeling that a plant needs care. I really think that one can walk into a room where there are plants which are loved and cared for regularly and sense if any one of them is in distress. It may be just that I have developed the habit of glancing at my plants when I enter a room (they are usually the loveliest things to be seen so the eye is naturally drawn to them), but, in that momentary glance, I am able to take in and assess their general air of well being. Some may call it "talking to your plants", but I'm sure that many will understand.

There are less esoteric ways of telling if a fern needs water. A fern should be watered when the moisture level is getting low for that particular plant's needs. This is indicated by the look and feel of the soil. An initial glance may tell that the soil is dry, but this is not a true guide. The surface may be quite dry, but a little below the surface the soil may feel cool and damp. You can test this with your finger without disturbing the roots too much, especially if the soil mix is soft. This kind of indication of moisture levels is good for both potted and free-growing plants. You can see all is well for that day and possibly the next, but that water may be needed the day after, depending on the weather.

A moisture meter is excellent for the job, but a trifle more expensive than the finger measure. Some people swear by the use of a smooth flat pebble placed on the soil on top of a pot. If there is condensation on the underside of the pebble there is still moisture in the soil. Another and most efficient way of telling if a plant should be watered is by the "feel" of the container. A pot that is getting on the dry side will feel light in comparison to one that has just been watered. If your plants are in big pots, of course this will be hard work to assess, so you can try the "sound" technique. A pot that is on the dry side will have a sharp ringing sound to it if lightly tapped on the side round about the middle. One that has plenty of moisture in it will sound dull. This technique works well for terracotta pots and a wooden instrument is best for sound reproduction.

How to Water

Potted ferns and ferns growing in the garden require very thorough soaking with a gentle flow of water. In the case of a potted plant, apply water until it is flowing freely through the drainage holes. In the garden, water must be allowed to soak well down into the soil. This deep watering is essential in the garden to encourage the roots to go down into the soil to seek water. It means that they anchor themselves more firmly and explore more food territory. Frequent light waterings encourage the roots to stay up near the soil surface where they are very vulnerable to drying out if a day's watering is missed, and to damage from cultivation, or the digging of cats and dogs. They miss out, too, on the readily available food in the deeper soil levels. In the case of a potted plant, this thorough watering ensures that moisture is distributed right through the soil, and into the root ball itself. It ensures that the fibrous, moisture-retentive components of the soil mixture are thoroughly wetted, thereby decreasing the number of times that watering has to be done. Thorough watering also ensures that the salts which build up in the soil through constant tap watering are flushed out. These salts often show up as a grey crystalline crust on the top of the soil. They should be scraped off and the soil watered by the above technique until it is "sweet" again and the toxic salts leached out.

To carry out this thorough watering technique in the garden, you need a gentle pressure on the hose through a fine rose nozzle. Hard, direct pressure will dislodge soil particles and mean constant replacing of top soil. The delicate, fibrous roots of ferns which are always close to the surface can be

damaged this way too.

A gentle hosing is effective for potted plants. They are, by the way, much easier to water if the plant has been potted so that the soil is at least 2 cm (1 in) below the rim. Pots can then be filled to the brim, allowed to drain, then filled again.

Soaking potted plants: Potted plants that are easily handled can be soaked in a tub of water. This is an effective method for wetting potting mixes that have completely dehydrated. Some commercial mixes have a great deal of fibre and plastic materials that are very hard to reconstitute. The exceptionally light mixes which will float away if submerged can be a nuisance. The best way to cope with this is to anticipate the problem and weigh the soil down with a cloth or stones.

It is not good for the fern to be left soaking too long; just soak it enough to ensure that the soil is wet through. If left too long, the water can become chilled and the roots deprived of oxygen for long enough to damage them.

Warnings

The fronds should not be overly wetted and allowed to stay wet—a gentle shake will remove the excess. Green parts that are wet and standing in the sunlight can develop dark burn spots where the droplets of water have intensified the effect of the sun's rays. Foliage should not stay wet overnight in the cold weather as it can freeze, or for any length of time in a very humid atmosphere because this encourages fungus and bacteria troubles.

Water should not be poured down the hole in the crown of a fern that develops a trunk, such as a tree fern. If wet for too long the soft woody tissue will rot and the embryonic fronds will not develop.

Effective draining is essential to a potted fern's well being. After watering, make sure that the water is flowing freely out of the drain holes in the bottom or sides of the pot. This can be done by standing the pot on a rack, or on sand or pebbles in a tray, or if they are house plants, leaving them outside in a sheltered place until they have stopped dripping.

If the pot normally stands in a saucer, do be sure that that any water that drains away from the pot does not accumulate in the saucer where it will be taken up again by the plant. The idea is to get rid of those toxic salts in the soil. For this reason also, water that accumulates in a saucer should never be tipped back over a plant.

In the garden effective drainage is essential too. The impression that one gets where ferns grow naturally is that the ground is always wet, but that water is constantly moving and being replenished by fresh water. So it should be in the garden. If the ground does not drain well, the accumulating water will become stagnant and the roots will rot away.

Rain

The most effective watering for potted plants is light showers of rain. The gentle drizzle will gently and thoroughly wash their fronds free of garden and house dust, and replace toxic salts in the soil with soft, fresh rainwater. Even a few hours of this treatment is a real tonic for them. Of course, the rain must be gentle and unaccompanied by wind and hail and other natural disasters.

Water Temperature

One of the nice things about rainwater is that it is usually warm, and a fern that is used to mild conditions like those in a glasshouse or indoors will enjoy the constant temperature. Water that is approximately the same temperature as the fern's surroundings should be used when hand watering or soaking plants. This can be done by standing the watering can in the same room as the ferns for a while so that the water is the same temperature as the room. Some nurserymen believe that this also allows any chemicals in tap water to settle or evaporate. It can be a tedious business if you have a lot of watering to do. A recommended range of temperatures is from 18°C (65°F) to 26°C (80°F)—as long as the water feels comfortable to touch. A sudden rush of cold water through the soil can give the roots a very real shock and set the plant back. The hot water from hoses left

lying in the sun can also damage even hardened fern growth.

Planting and transplanting

When any plant is moved from the place or pot in which it is growing, it is given quite a shock, no matter how carefully handled. Such a shock means that some roots are lost and the delicate root hairs which are the plant's feeding systems are dislodged or bruised on the remaining roots. The plant must replace these, repair damaged tissues, re-anchor itself, and at the same time, upstairs parts must adjust to new surroundings and resume normal operations. So moving day should be made as easy on the plant as possible.

Hardening

Potted plants can be prepared for new ground quarters by being left to stand for a few days in the area in which they are to be planted. This gives the green parts time to adjust gradually to new light and air conditions, and will give the whole plant a good start when actually put into the soil.

Plants that you buy these days are rarely hardened before sale, as they once were. Nurserymen used to have a kind of halfway house where plants stayed for a week or two, to get used to the tougher conditions of the outside world after the soft life that they had led in the glasshouse. Now only very conscientious growers do this.

A great many failures that people have with potted house plants, ferns in particular, are due to this neglect. Plants are turned over so quickly that one that was in the glasshouse yesterday, is in someone's garden or windowbox today, desperately trying to catch up on what has happened to it in the past twenty-four hours. Straight from the usually heated glasshouse, ferns are just too soft, and too vulnerable to change. When buying a new plant, try to ensure that the nurseryman deals with a reputable grower, or at least be aware that the plants he buys are not hardened, and that he is treating them accordingly. Be sure that the plant selected has not been sitting in the dark in the back of the nursery for a few days, or standing in a draughty place.

Planting

Ferns with creeping rhizomes: This includes such plants as the Polypodiums and Davallias, which should be planted so that the rhizome rests lightly on the soil and the fibrous roots are firmly and completely covered. The tip should be pointing in the direction you wish it to take.

Ferns with erect rhizomes: Ferns such as Aspleniums and Blechnums should be planted so that the crown is just level with the soil surface. These species which are caudescent (i.e. which form a caudex or pseudo-trunk) should have the old dead parts of the caudex pared away with a sharp knife until living tissue is exposed, then the whole should be planted so that the crown is level with the soil. Unless paring is done, the tissues will not be stimulated sufficiently to produce enough new growth to support such an established plant, and it may die.

Young, soft-tissued ferns: These should be planted so that the original soil level is maintained. Any lower and the stems will rot; any higher will mean that that area of the root zone above the ground will not be able to function.

Epiphytic ferns: The care of epiphytic ferns is very much the same as that for terrestrial ferns, but extra attention must be paid to the drainage of the medium in which the plant grows, whether it is in the ground or in a pot. Bear in mind that an epiphyte fern grows naturally on another plant, usually fairly high on a tree or on another tall-growing fern. Under these conditions the roots function in the accumulated humus in the bark, fibre or crevices of the host plant and this humus is never wet for any length of time—in fact it can become quite dry in between rainfalls. So, in the ground the soil should drain readily or agricultural drains should be installed, or the plant moved to higher ground. In a pot extra grit in the potting mixture and perhaps an extra layer of crocks in the bottom will permit water to flow through quickly, or more importantly not accumulate and encourage a soggy state in the soil. Watering should be done when the soil—in ground or pot—is on the dry side of moist.

Clay pots with large drain holes and wire or wood baskets lined with natural materials like bark, moss or coconut fibre are better for epiphyte ferns than those made with plastic. These natural materials are porous and allow the air to circulate through the potting mixture and around the roots, so that the plant is growing in something that is close to its natural state.

Transplanting

A fern's dormant time is *not* the time to move it: it must be actively growing during early spring and late autumn. In temperate areas, if midsummer conditions are prevailingly dry, planting should be put off. In tropical areas, if sure that growth has not stopped, a fern can be moved any time.

Transplant ferns only when healthily growing

Potted plants and smaller ferns: A potted plant should be watered the day before planting as it is easier to remove from the pot when damp, and there is less likelihood of dry soil coming away from the root ball and taking tiny roots and root hairs with it. If woody roots have been broken in transferring operations, they should be cut off cleanly with a sharp knife or secateurs and in the case of dire root damage, a compensating amount of top growth should also be removed as near to the crown as possible.

Moving larger ferns: Before lifting a big fern that is bound to have a dense root ball, leave the hose to soak gently on it for a day or two. Like a plant in a pot, it is easier and safer to remove when the soil is damp. A very large fern such as a tree fern should have a trench dug around it 45 cm (18 in) from the trunk. It should then be left as long as possible — preferably the growing season before you intend to move it, so that it can make new roots close to the trunk. This root pruning is best carried out in early spring while growth is at its peak. The trench should be dug with a sharp spade that severs the roots cleanly to a depth of at least 30 cm (12 in). Fill this trench with loose fibrous material and grit to encourage new root development at this point, so that when moved, new roots are already forming and ready to spread out into the new territory. This is not necessary for the *Dicksonia antarctica*, which transplants easily when the trunk is sawn through at any

To loosen ferns before moving from larger pots, place a piece of cloth on the side of the pot and gently tap it with a mallet

point. But it is a useful method if as much height as possible is to be retained.

Fertilisers

There is a theory that fertilising a fern accelerates its growth and shortens its life span. A handful of old cow manure, blood and bone or leaf mould, while ferns are growing in spring and summer, should be all that they need. But, if even more and even greener luxurious fronds are what you want, then by all means fertilise them. But do it very carefully, following the instructions on the packet scrupulously, and in the case of your favourite and precious plants, halving the recommended dose. The nearer the approach to natural conditions that is provided for ferns, the greater will be the success and the fewer the disappointments.

Nitrogen is the nutrient most needed by ferns, but a complete and balanced fertiliser is probably best to use in the garden and for a potted plant. Straight chemicals (such as sulphate of ammonia to supplement nitrogen) tend to throw out the soil chemistry, which can take a long time and a lot of energy to rectify. A complete fertiliser is one that contains the three main plant foods, nitrogen (N), phosphorus (P) and potash (K). An incomplete fertiliser is one that contains only one or two of these foods. Both fertilisers come in organic and inorganic, liquid and dry forms. Some are fast release, some are slow release. All commercially made fertilisers must carry an analysis of their contents somewhere on the container, so it is possible to work out how "complete" or how "balanced" a particular product is. Commercial products advertised as having "low burn" properties are recommended for ferns as it means that the fertiliser contains fewer soluble salts which cause burning.

Organic Fertilisers

Organic fertilisers are of animal or vegetable origin, often derived from slaughter houses, refuse and vegetable wastes such as seed residues. They mainly contain nitrogen in the form of protein, which soil organisms quickly change into nitrates for a plant's use.

Animal wastes often contain bone residue which provides phosphates; some also contain potash as well as some trace elements. (Trace elements are the minor foods that all plants need in small quantities.)

Organic fertilisers can be given in the form of blood and bone, hoof and horn meal, fish meal, castor meal and wood ashes. Leaf mould, compost and manure, also excellent natural fertilisers, have been discussed already as more soil conditioners than food supplements. Leaf mould is the most balanced of them all, being an ideal fertiliser and soil conditioner.

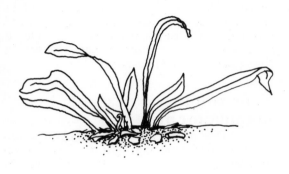

Compost, leaf mould and manure are excellent natural fertilisers for ferns

Blood and bone: This is processed meat meal which contains 5-6 per cent nitrogen, and from 10-14 per cent phosphoric acid. This is often confused with dried blood and bone dust fertilisers, both of which are suited to fern culture. Dried blood has a fast sustained action if the soil is warm: bone dust supplies a slow and steady flow of nutrients depending on the grade of the particles. Dried blood, however, contains many soluble salts and should be used very carefully for ferns.

Hoof and horn: Hoof and horn is useful in potting mixtures because of its coarse consistency. Its 12 per cent nitrogen content is readily available to plants and has a long-lasting effect.

Fish meal: Fish meal (5-10 per cent nitrogen, 2-6 per cent phosphoric acid) usually consists of fish wastes combined with inorganic fertilisers and is sold as fish manures. They act quickly, giving a sustained supply of nitrogen and phosphorus, but should not be used as a sole and continual food supplement for ferns as they build up the alkalies in the soil. Fish manures are balanced fertilisers—all the major foods are contained in them in balanced proportions.

Wood ash: A rich source of potash, but wood ashes vary according to the materials burnt. Hardwood is the greatest source. However, too great a build-up of ashes in the soil of a fern bed, makes it too alkaline for the plants' well being.

Inorganic Fertilisers

Unless very carefully applied, inorganic fertilisers derived from chemicals or mining processes can give a concentrated amount of food in a very brief period. This encourages a sudden burst of growing, producing very rank growth that is very vulnerable to any hardship. For example, a heavy dose of nitrogen in the form of hoof and horn meal can safely be given to a fern bed, but the equivalent amount, in the form of nitrate of soda, would be devastating—everything will grow like mad for a while, making a lot of lush, very fragile growth, or be completely burned away.

Fertiliser Forms

Fertiliser comes in dry, liquid, tablet and slow-release granule forms. It does not matter to ferns in what form it comes, provided it is administered carefully. The actual form of the plant food is probably more a case of what suits the budget and convenience, rather than what is best for the fern.

Generally, concentrates in small bottles, tablets wrapped in individual plastic containers, and dry forms in elaborate dispensers are expensive but they are also very convenient. Bulk lots of liquid and dry foods are cheaper, but be sure that you can use them all within the prescribed time. Some fertilisers can change in composition if they are kept for very long periods, or deteriorate significantly in quality. Check with the manufacturer before you invest in a bulk lot.

Liquid, tablet and slow-release granules are very easy to use. Their quantities are easy to measure and the liquid kind distributes evenly through the soil. There is less likelihood of an accidental overdose burning roots and foliage if the food is in a liquid form, but then, there is considerable waste in run off and by-passing of the root zones.

Tablets tend to concentrate the areas fertilized unevenly, and delicate fern roots can be damaged by this. Tablets and granules tend to disperse rather quicker than the manufacturers intended, for they are water soluble, and the more frequent watering required by ferns than other plants breaks them down quickly. Sometimes too quickly for ferns, and again, they can be burned.

Care and time will be necessary to spread dry fertiliser evenly over the soil — mixing it with dry sand makes this an easier task — and prevent it touching the fern fronds, particularly any new fronds. It is especially important in the case of ferns that form a crown, to prevent the tiniest amount from settling there. Fertiliser should be distributed on damp ground and then watered in thoroughly. The disadvantages of dry fertilisers lie in the amount of fussing that must go into their application: their advantages are that they are cheap and last longer in the soil than do water soluble plant foods.

It is, of course, a waste of time and money to feed a fern that is not growing, or is entering its dormant period. The food will only be washed out of the soil with routine watering.

Words of Warning

After fertilisation, oncoming growth needs careful watching. Sometimes this very tender part of the plant burns and withers away, while the rest of the foliage picks up and really looks good. If the new growth is killed off this way a few times in a row, the plant will not be able to replenish itself and will run out of puff and die. This is often the reason for the inexplicable demise of a plant that otherwise seemed to be thriving.

Another warning: don't automatically feed a fern that looks sick without first checking for other adverse conditions, like waterlogged soil, poor ventilation or insufficient light. Repotted, breathing freely, or in a brighter place and growing again, it can then be given a very gentle dose of ideal medicine, like leaf mould, to help it along.

If fertilising has been overdone, there is hope for the plant if signs of burning are detected quickly — the leaves will go brown and brittle. The excess chemicals can be washed out by flooding the plant or the pot with water over and over again, then allowing it to drain well. A change of soil, gentle repotting — so that the roots do not get yet another shock — and careful nursing might also help. An older fern with woody roots or rhizome and a tough trunk may be able to cope with such treatment and recover, a young plant probably cannot.

Year round management

One of the nicest things about ferns is their undemanding nature. They keep growing in the same spot in the garden and in the same old pot, year in and year out. They do not need forcing or holding back (horrible things to do to any plant), they do not have to be dug up and stored like prize dahlias, fussed over like orchids and preened like giant chrysanthemums. They will not have tantrums like roses do if asked to grow with something less beautiful than themselves, or turn their lovely heads away if asked to grow alongside vulgar hybrids, some of whose colours and shapes must surely offend the elegant and restrained ferns. Instead they spread out and embrace, and lend their softening air, making everything around them easier on the eye.

Spring

In early spring when lengthening days signal growing time to the embryonic fiddleheads, they ask only for more water and a new mulch of leaf mould or old cow manure. They like, too, to have the old fronds that have weathered the winter removed if they threaten to crowd the new fast-emerging ones. These early fronds need protection from sudden cold winds that linger from winter days and sudden hot gusts that capricious spring can bring.

Aphids and people are a fern's worst spring enemies. If the new fronds are damaged, you will have to put up with them until the next growing season, so fend off people who want to touch the new growth, and look for the aphids which may be hard see against the dark new growth, and destroy them.

Summer

In the summer, potted and basket ferns will need extra protection from dehydration and hot dry winds. Some that have revelled in a situation that gets gentle spring sunlight, may need moving to shadier quarters as the sun climbs higher in the sky and its rays become harsher. Hot winds dehydrate baskets (cold winds in winter do too), and heat reflected off tin fences and brick walls will burn a fern's delicate growth at this time of the year. Hot sun beating down on the sides of a terracotta or plastic pot can devastate what is inside, but if potted plants are grouped together, they afford some protection to each other. Or one pot placed inside a moss-lined, larger pot forms a very effective summertime protection. Baskets

and pots that have been put under a tree for extra protection may need watering—it may have rained in the night, but the tree is a giant umbrella.

Lots and lots of leaf mould and cool mulches are what is needed at this time of the year to keep the roots cool and cut down moisture loss through evaporation. However, it is best to keep the damp mulches away from stems and rhizomes in a very humid atmosphere as this may encourage fungus growth.

Autumn

New fronds may continue to appear until early autumn, but after that growth will slow down and ferns of the temperate areas will shut up shop for the winter ahead. Deciduous ferns will yellow and shed their fronds. Those that retain their leaves should be left alone, no matter how tatty they look, as removal of these fronds (which may still be working and needed) may encourage new growth that is not hardy enough to get through the winter's cold. These old fronds will protect the past season's growth, and the trunk, if the fern is in an exposed place over winter.

No need to feed the plants now, and watering in pots and in the ground should be cut down.

Old mulches can be left in place because the spores will have fallen by now, and if you look closely you may find tiny green prothalli forming under sheltering fronds. They will establish before the cold winter months and be well settled in to make the most of spring growing time.

Winter

Ferns get through winter days without demanding much of their keepers at all. The deciduous ones go completely dormant, asking only to be left alone and for their soil to be kept on the dry side of moist. Semideciduous ones and those of the temperate areas which have been asked to live in colder places, ask only to be protected from frost and tolerated while they are not looking their best.

PROPAGATION AND HYBRIDISING
4

The propagation of ferns is not a great gardening mystery, nor is it something too technical or too time consuming for the home gardener. It is a slow but interesting and rewarding process, and makes economic sense if many ferns are wanted.

New ferns can be raised in two ways—by vegetative means, or by sexual means from the spores. Both are very simple.

Vegetative methods are carried out by division, planting or layering of bulbils, auricle cuttings, meristem culture and apospory or apogamy.

Division

A great many ferns are very easily increased by division—it is in fact the only way that some fern cultivars can be increased, as many of them are sterile or do not come true from spores. Ferns which form creeping surface rhizomes or root stocks, for example Davallias and Polypodiums, can be cut up cleanly—not broken or torn—into 5-8 cm (2-3 in) portions if they have a growing tip or living tissues, and these portions used to form new plants.

Dead tissue is cut away, damaged roots are trimmed, old and excess fronds removed and the pieces replanted at their original level in a potting mixture containing a lot of fibre and grit which enables newly formed roots to penetrate quickly and easily.

The rhizome of epiphyte ferns, such as some *Asplenium* species, is best placed in sphagnum moss and leaf mould, rather than a mixture containing soil, as it is closer to their natural condition.

In the case of plants which form crowns, for example Blechnums and Polystichums, division propagation can be carried out when the plant has built up a number of these. Strong growing crowns are removed by slicing them off the mother plant with a sharp knife, ensuring that each plantlet has sufficient living tissue and roots to survive. These pieces are put into a well-drained propagating mixture containing a lot of grit and fibre in a pot just big enough to contain the roots.

Layering Bulbils

Plants that form colonies in their natural state, like the *Asplenium bulbiferum, Polystichum proliferum* and *Woodwardia radicans*, often carry a great many plantlets or bulbils on their fronds along the rachis (midrib) or on the tip of the frond, as a kind of accessory reproduction system. At first these are evident as small scaly knobs, then as embryonic fronds which gradually, as the frond matures, are forced down into closer contact with the soil by the pressure of new growth forming at the centre of the plant. When they come into contact with soil, roots develop and the miniature plant, a true sporophyte, is ready for independent growth after the supporting frond has withered away.

To encourage this growth of new plants, the mature bulbil-bearing frond is pegged down onto a damp propagating mix in a pot or seedling box until independent growth is obvious. The frond is then separated from the parent and allowed to rot away. Alternatively, the larger bulbils are clipped off together with a small portion of the parent frond and planted in a seed box. This is kept thoroughly misted until the plant shows signs of independent growth.

Plantlets or bulbils growing from an *Asplenium* frond

Bulbil production of another kind can sometimes be encouraged in an old plant of *Asplenium scolopendrium* where the old frond base often remains green and fleshy long after—sometimes years after—the fronds have withered. The old fronds can be broken away close to the main stock of the plant, trimmed of any dead matter and laid firmly in damp grit and fibre propagating mixture where, after a few weeks, they may produce up to a dozen white bulbils which can be removed and planted out separately. The remains of the stock plant can be trimmed of dead tissue and replanted lower into the soil with a few fronds left at the top. This often has the effect of rejuvenating an old plant.

Offsets and Auricle Tips

Offsets are formed by some of the tree-like ferns of the *Blechnum, Dicksonia* and *Cyathea* genera and new plants can be propagated from these offsets. The offset is cut from the parent plant with a sharp knife and an almost equal amount of the parent tissue taken with it. This is potted in a "thumb pot" which is a nurseryman's term for a tiny terracotta pot about 5 cm (2 in) in diameter, or a plastic "tube" pot. The ideal propagation mixture should be rich in sharp sand for drainage and to stimulate the tissues into producing roots. Once planted the offsets must be kept moist and a glass bell jar or a plastic covering will help prevent dehydration of the foliage. New plants are often disappointingly slow to start.

Two genera, *Angiopteris* and *Marattia*, produce fleshy, ear-like protuberances on the rhizome below the stipe or stem base. These can be cut away and planted so that the auricle tip, as it is called, is just above the soil. In time one, and sometimes two, new plants may develop.

Meristem Culture

Meristem culture or tissue culture is highly scientific, involving autoclaves and laboratory-like equipment, and is best left to commercial growers who produce plants in thousands. Orchids and lately ferns are being mass-produced in this way. The process is revolutionising commercial wholesale growing and in some instances where plants, such as those in the *Nephrolepis* genus, are particularly suited to this propagation method, spore-raising houses are being phased out.

A tiny piece of tissue is removed from a mature stock parent plant, sterilised, placed in a growth stimulating and maintaining solution and sealed in a flask. As growths are produced they are separated from the parent tissue and placed in larger sealed containers. When growth is about 2 cm (1 in) high—after about three months—the mericlone, as it is now called, is placed in seedling boxes and cared for in the open glasshouse. Because the tissue is removed from adult plants and the cells are matured chemically, growth is twice that of seedling plants and within a year the mericlone has the appearance of a well-grown advanced plant. Plant tissue culture is in its infancy so far and not yet extended as a propagation method, but for the commercial grower it is a highly efficient, if initially very expensive, way to get new plants. But the buyer must be aware that he is buying a forced plant, used to hothouse treatment and probably not hardened in the old-fashioned nurseryman's sense.

Apospory and Apogamy

Some ferns and fern varieties, for example *Polystichum setiferum* var. *pulcherrimum*, reproduce themselves by very strange non-sexual methods called apospory and apogamy.

Apospory development is when the prothallus grows directly out of a deformed spore capsule or directly from a frond or pinna, rather like a bulbil, but this is a first generation prothallus not a second generation sporophyte.

Apogamy development is when a young fern is produced from a bud on the prothallus without sexual fertilisation having taken place within the prothallus. *Pteris cretica* and *Cyrtomium falcatum* are examples of ferns that can develop in this way. This kind of growth results from a spore which is self-fertile, that is, one which contains the requisite number of chromosomes for growth.

Growth from both apospory and

apogamy development can be cultivated by pegging the frond bearing the growth onto a damp propagating mix and keeping the immediate atmosphere warm and moist.

The above vegetative propagation methods are best done in warmer months of the year when plants are growing actively, and the forming, or newly formed, plants kept under glass, preferably with bottom heat, until well established. A sterile, evenly damp propagating soil mixture, clean pots, high and constant humidity, softly filtered light and very gentle handling of baby plants will help avoid disappointments.

Spore Culture

Spore culture, despite long dissertations you may read and take fright at, is a simple and rather interesting procedure. However, there are a few things that really must be carried out with care, otherwise all efforts will be in vain.

The pans, containers, soil mix and utensils used should be scrupulously clean and scalded, water should be boiled or pure rainwater used, and every process should be carried out as speedily as possible. These precautions must be taken to exclude the growth of algae, fungi, liverworts and mosses which thrive in the same conditions that the prothalli need to grow and which usually overwhelm the delicate prothallial growth.

There are several ways of going about spore raising but the following is a fairly simple and traditional method. From midsummer onwards the spores are collected from a mature frond which still holds sporangia that appear to be ripe. You may need a magnifying glass to see this. Check that all the sporangia are still intact and have not opened and already shed their spores — spore cases will have a ragged look if they have already opened.

Collection is done easily by snipping off a promising piece of frond, laying it between a folded piece of clean white paper and keeping it in a warm, dry place. After a few days the sporangia will have opened and shed their spores, which appear as fine dust on the paper. The spores are then gently tapped onto a smaller piece of paper which is folded as a protection until sowing starts.

The sooner the spores are sown, the better will be the results. The viable period of spores varies greatly. Some like the spores of *Osmunda* genus lose their viability within days. Others like the spores of *Todea* and *Leptopteris* genera lose their viability within hours. Though the spores of most other genera remain viable for longer, sometimes years, it is better to err on the side of caution and sow as quickly as possible.

Sterilising equipment: Shallow pans or pots of terracotta or plastic should be thoroughly cleaned and scalded with boiling water. Pots are then filled with a layer first of drainage material and then chopped sphagnum moss, peat moss, tree fern fibre or commercial seed raising mixture. This should be sterilised by pouring boiling water over and through it. A piece of netting or muslin over the top of the pot will stop the mixture from flooding over the sides while the water is being poured. After sterilisation the pot should immediately be covered with a sheet of glass or plastic film so that uninvited fungi and moss spores do not settle on it.

When the growing medium has cooled the spores are spread as evenly as possible over the surface and then covered quickly with glass or plastic. Spores are easier to spread if they are mixed with washed fine sand.

Watering: The pot is plunged into a container of clean water and the growing medium thoroughly dampened then drained. Boiled or rain water should again be used and the medium kept on the wet side of moist. The cover is left on the pot until embryonic fronds appear. If removed earlier it could permit the entry of dangerous foreign organisms.

The pots containing spores can be placed in a shady protected situation and any time from four weeks to six months later a fine green scum formed by the developing prothalli will become evident. Several weeks after these first visible signs the prothalli's distinctive heart shape is obvious and a few weeks later the first true embryonic fronds will appear.

At this stage the cover can be removed from the pot and the plants gradually hardened and pricked out if they are big enough to handle. "Pricking out" means lifting, separating and spacing out individual plants — a rather tedious and time-consuming job but very necessary if the plants are to develop without a struggle. Pricking out will be difficult if the spores have not been sown evenly. It requires a steady hand and much patience but the tiny plants will stand a fair amount of handling as long as the roots do not dry out.

It may take as long as two years before new plants are ready to go in 10 cm (4 in) pots. A few mature fronds should have formed and the root ball developed to a stage where it almost fills the pot.

Another simple and conventional sowing method is to stuff a sterilised terracotta pot with sphagnum moss and invert it in a saucer of water. Spores are sown onto the base of the pot and the whole covered with a bell jar. A brick standing in water and covered with a bell jar does a similar kind of job though the brick should first be sterilised with boiling water to kill any unwanted spores.

Hybridising

Hybridisation does not happen in nature very often, nor is it something that the average fern grower indulges in. However, there is a simple "hit and miss" method and a very exacting scientific method, both of which are interesting if time-consuming. For each method success is more likely if the two ferns come from closely related genera.

The "simple" method involves sowing the mixed spores of the two plants thickly together in the same pot. The pot is then doused with a fine jet of water daily for several days when the prothalli are at the stage of fertilisation. Alternatively the prothalli can be just submerged in luke-warm water and the water gently swirled around the pot several times a day for two or three days. It must be done this often as the sexual organs of each species may mature on different days.

To determine if the prothalli are mature enough to release sperm involves inspection through a microscope — a magnifying glass is not powerful enough. The male organs (antheridia) and the female organs (archegonia) are situated in different parts of the prothallus — the archegonia at the "notch" in the heart shaped prothallus and the antheridia on the lower or basal part of the plant. The neck of the archegonium opens when the egg cells are ready to be fertilised and the sperm-activating substance, malic acid, is released.

The more scientific approach to hybridisation involves some surgery. The spores of the two ferns to be crossed are sown in separate pans and when the prothalli are ready to be fertilised, the male parts are cut away with a razor blade or scalpel from each prothallus and switched over to the other pan, being placed close to, or overlapping the remaining female portions of the prothalli. Again the soil should be kept awash for several days.

Generally the spores from hybrid plants are sterile and any propagation is done by vegetative methods.

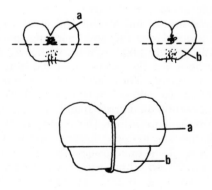

A method of hybridising ferns. The notched end is cut off the intended female parent (a) and the tapered end cut off the intended male parent (b). These are then overlapped, planted and kept well watered for several days

PESTS AND DISEASES
5

Humans are probably a fern's worst enemies. I know of no other pest which can cause such devastation by neglect and ill treatment. Ferns hate over-handling, unfavourable situations, over-watering, over-spraying and over-feeding and all too often they are subjected to all these indignities. In two short weeks no nasty aphid, creepy mealy bug, ravenous slug or greasy scale could accomplish as much havoc as human "care"—no matter in what plague proportions they came. However, they hardly ever come in plague proportions and there is no need to worry that your entire fern collection is threatened if you see a leaf with a hole in it or a slightly droopy frond. There is no need to head for the nearest can of "kill everything in sight" and there is no need for diligent monthly or seasonal spray programmes. You only have to take the time and the trouble to look closely to see what is happening.

A wan appearance may not be due to a pest or disease. More common causes are waterlogged soil or soil which is dry and caked and will not absorb water, draughts in corners, or too moist or too dry an atmosphere, or the plants may be root bound. If you are sure that all these systems are functioning well, take a hand lens and look closely at the ailing fern.

Places to look are under the fronds, along the stems, in the furry corners where the stems meet, and at the soil level where the stem goes into the soil. Sucking insects like scale, mealy bug, aphids, white fly and leaf hoppers are the pests most likely to be found on ferns. They are, on the whole, responsible for discoloration and lack of vigour in established growth and distortion of new growth. To confuse the issue, all these sucking insects secrete a large amount of honey dew. This encourages the growth of sooty mould so that the leaves become covered with a black, greasy, powdery substance and the creature initially responsible is not easily seen.

Ants

Where there is black mould, usually there will be ants as well. The ants actually hatch and tend the eggs of sucking insects and carry them to the plant where they milk them for their honeydew. They also carry baby insects from one plant to another so a new plant will very quickly become infected too. Both ants and sucking insects should be eradicated.

Scale

Scale appears as small greasy lumps, some brown, some grey and some, when very young, a milky white. They tend to collect on stems and on the underside of leaves, where they are often mistaken for sori. Mild infestations can be controlled by constant removal with the fingers, or wiping or spraying the fronds with a mild soapy water solution or a weak solution of white oil and water—100 mL (4 fl oz) of white oil per 4.5 L (1 gal) of water. This may need to be repeated at two-week intervals for a while as the young continue to hatch from under the older scale or are brought by the ants. A weak solution is recommended for ferns as white oil tends to stunt growth if used several times over a few weeks.

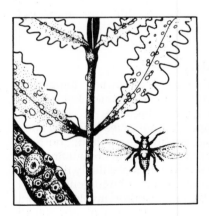

Aphids

Aphids are fleshy-bodied little insects, some with wings, which are green, brown and black. Looking somewhat like fleas, they cluster on the new growth and feed off it, especially in spring, so that when it unfurls it is grossly distorted. If you are concerned about using toxic sprays, aphids can be dealt with by spraying them off the foliage with a jet of water. Most of them will land on the ground where they will be eaten by ground-foraging insects. Few will have the fortitude to climb back up again. Small infestations can be sprayed with a soap and water solution. Low toxicity sprays such as pyrethrum or maldison can be used in mild concentrations—about half the concentration recommended by the manufacturer—to deal with heavy infestations.

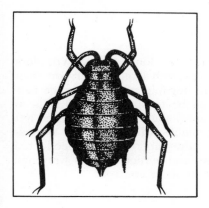

Mealy Bugs

Mealy bugs are little horrors and the most difficult of the sucking insects to deal with. The bugs are greyish-white and have a cotton wool-like or meal-like texture. A lot of them together look quite soft and fluffy, but they are devils. Malathion and white oil combined in a weak solution will be effective if they have taken a hold in the glasshouse or

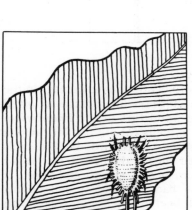

shade house. If they are present on only a few potted plants, a useful old remedy is to touch each one with a cotton wool-tipped stick dipped in a solution of half methylated spirits and half water. The areas where a lot of stems join trucks and a lot of stems cluster thickly should also be treated—the bugs are bound to be there.

White Fly

Greenhouse white flies resemble miniature moths with very white wings. They form in clusters on the underside of leaves. Though they do not do too much damage to vigorous plants, they can be effectively controlled with pyrethrum-based sprays or a mixture of white oil and malathion.

Leaf Hoppers

Leaf hoppers are recognisable by their hopping action. The passion-vine leaf

hopper is a definite menace among ferns, both adult and juvenile forms causing damage to young fronds. It is hard to eradicate the very mobile colonies, but they can be subdued with constant spraying of pyrethrum and malathion in a half-strength solution.

Caterpillars

Caterpillar, snail and slug damage is immediately obvious. Small infestations of caterpillars can be controlled by removing them with the fingers or spraying them with carbaryl.

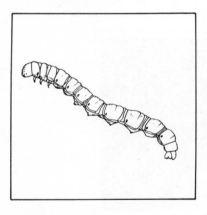

Snails and Slugs

Snails and slugs leave silvery trails which are a giveaway. They come out at night and after the rain so can be anticipated and

caught. Alternatively they can be trapped in flowerpots filled with lettuce leaves left lying on their sides in the garden or in the fern house. It is a good idea to check the undersides of pots where slugs and small snails may congregrate in the drain holes, and any dark, moist corners among the staging of the fern house or the rocks of the rock garden. Proprietary brand baits are effective, but dangerous if there are small children and pets around.

Earwigs

Earwigs are long, segmented, dark brown creatures with large pincers on their tails. They are horrible and can damage new fronds but can be trapped in small rolls of furled newspaper, slightly dampened and left lying amidst plants where damage is suspected. The newspapers can be collected every few days and burned till this wretched little creature is under control.

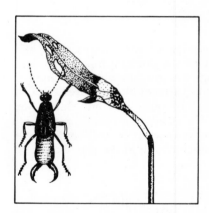

Staghorn Beetles

Staghorn beetles cause damage in the form of brown shot-hole-like pittings followed by wilt to the frond tips of the *Platycerium* species. They actually eat out regular cavities in the upper surface of the fronds. The adult beetles lay their eggs in the new tips so these parts can be crushed or cut off and burnt. If the damage is bad and widespread on big ferns, the adult beetles can be controlled with a derris or pyrethrum spray.

Grouped to protect each other and to enjoy the trapped humidity are
Adiantum raddianum var. *variegatum tesselata, Adiantum raddianum* cv. Pacific Maid,
Adiantum raddianum cv. Fragrans, *Nephrolepis exaltata* cv. Verona
and *Lygodium japonicum*

Top: A catchpot filled with damp sphagnum moss keeps the atmosphere
sufficiently humid for this *Adiantum* species
Bottom left: Ferns perfectly complement this period setting
Bottom right: Contrasting *Adiantum* and *Blechnum* species in matching
jardinieres make an attractive decorating feature

Top: A decorative way to show off the furry feet of *Davallia mariesii*
Bottom: *Asplenium nidus*. When grown this way in a pot,
careful attention must be paid to drainage of the soil mix

Top left: *Asplenium* species
Top right: *Adiantum capillus-veneris* cv. Imbricatum
Bottom: *Arachniodes aristata variegatum*

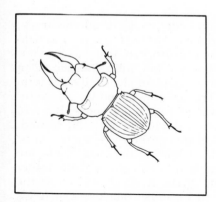

Eel Worms

Eel worms, which are microscopic nematodes, damage foliage during the cooler months, causing patches of red-brown and black between the veins. They are hard to cope with because watering helps spread them when it splashes around. The infected plant should be isolated and preferably destroyed, but if it is a favourite which must be saved, the very toxic spray Lebacid can be used effectively at weekly intervals till all is clear.

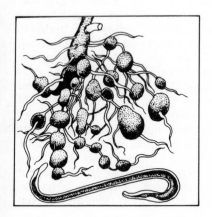

Diseases

There are very few diseases that affect ferns. Those that do are of fungous or bacterial origin and appropriate sprays arrest the trouble but rarely cure it. Infected plants and soil should be discarded and pots, tools and staging disinfected.

Ferns only succumb to these diseases if the conditions are suitable for bacterial and fungous growth, such as overly wet conditions for too long, foliage like the finely divided dense fronds of the *Nephrolepis* genus being wet too frequently, and a lack of air flow among crowded plants.

The diseases show up as black and brown spots with fine, hairy growths on them, or as rusty, powdery, and grey smutty patches on leaves and stems. Some fungus diseases grow on the honeydew secretions of leaf-sucking insects as mentioned earlier. They do no immediate harm to the plant but if allowed to spread will exclude enough light from the plant to be harmful. They disappear when the insect source is dealt with and the fronds are washed with a mild soap solution.

To Spray or Not to Spray

As an overall comment on sprays and insecticides, sometimes the cure is worse than the cause. Pests may be eliminated down to the last of their kind but the end result may be a plant with burnt and withered fronds, and one that is severely set back, not to say what damage can be self-inflicted by inhaling a lungful of malathion or covering the skin with carbaryl.

A point to bear in mind if you are concerned about the effect the actual spraying may have on yourself and the atmosphere, is that a toxic solution can be made up in a bucket and plants syringed, or the foliage of small potted plants can be dipped into the solution.

The manufacturer's instructions should always be followed (though the quantities given can often be halved) and protective covering should be worn. A plant that is in dry soil, is sick, or is standing in full sunlight, should not be sprayed, and spraying on windy days is ill-advised—goodness knows where the spray will end up. If the whole business can be avoided by using traps or spending a little time doing routine spot checks, learning the little creatures' habits and anticipating any trouble that they will make—then so much the better for everyone. As an overall precautionary measure take a tip from some nurserymen and hang a pest strip, such as Shelltox, among the indoor or greenhouse plants.

GROWING SITUATIONS
6

A fern garden outside, a fern garden inside, in the ground or in pots — wherever it is, it is bound to be lovely, if planted with the aspect and prevailing conditions in mind and given the simple care it needs. However, for most situations in which ferns are grown, there are hazards to guard against, routines to establish and methods to counteract growing conditions which are not ideal.

In the garden

A fern growing in an average suburban garden has many needs because the average suburban garden is not its natural state. It can be, though, the closest a fern grower can get to this state if plants of the temperate areas are cultivated in temperate areas and tropical plants are cultivated in tropical areas.

Positioning

It is such a common mistake to believe that ferns should be positioned under trees. The trouble is that, over the years, the trees will grow up and out, and if they are evergreen, cast heavy shade all year round. Their roots will encroach on and swamp the ferns' territory, so that food is scarce. Trees also act as great umbrellas, so that only the most penetrating rain falls on the fern beds underneath, to wash the fronds, dampen the earth and leach accumulating soil salts. The ferns may lie in the path of a penetrating wind once the trees' branches are high off the ground. The wind may be cold and constant and may blow away the ferns' natural mulch and food of accumulating leaves, so that the soil around them is bare and eroded. To complete the sad story, green flies may infest the trees, dropping their honeydew secretions on the ferns below, so that sooty mould takes a hold on old growth and is threatening what new growth is maintained under these very rugged conditions.

If you are planning a new garden or a fern bed in your existing garden, plan around the trees, not under them. For ferns are happier in a tree's dappled shade and away from its overwhelming competition for food and water. In a new garden they will be fine for a few years under young deciduous trees, and will continue to thrive if the tree roots do not invade their territory, or if shade does not become too heavy. They will relish the fallen leaves which accumulate plentifully and form a natural leaf mould mulch, and the rainwater which reaches the fronds and roots. If a fern bed under an established tree is desired, pockets of soil among the trees' roots can be dug out without hurting the tree. These are filled with a soft loam and grit mixture, rather like a potting mixture, which will allow the ferns' roots to establish quickly. The tree's roots will head for this lovely new territory, but the ferns will have had time to establish themselves. Ferns in these kinds of pockets will need regular mulching with leaf mould and old cow manure, so that the roots can feed near the top layers of soil and humus.

Aspect: If there is no dense shade cast by trees and buildings, a southerly aspect in the Southern Hemisphere, and a northerly aspect in the Northern Hemisphere, should be very good. If either of these aspects falls along the side of a house, or at the base of a fence, there is often not sufficient sunlight for flowering plants. Woody shrubs and herbaceous plants become lean and lank as they head off in search of sunlight, and this part of the garden is forgotten or avoided because it is ugly and useless. As most ferns are content to sit around in these usually cool, moist places that get little sunlight but plenty of reflected and natural light, you can plan a fern garden there that will hide ugly fences, block out unlovely views or simply act as a cool retreat on hot summer days. If this aspect tends towards the east, and your ferns get gentle morning sunlight, it should be just about ideal. If it is inclined to the west, provision for shade from the long, hot rays of the afternoon sun may be needed. In high summer, the sun's rays can unexpectedly sneak around corners and are often sufficiently strong to scorch new fronds.

A completely eastern aspect can be ideal too, as long as the sunlight does not stay on the bed for more than a few early morning hours. In the winter, longer periods of sun would suit many of the hardy species, but in the summer, late morning sun may be too strong for even these ferns. They may cope if watered well, but their growth will not be soft and pleasing to the eye.

If any aspect chosen is totally shaded all the time, and gets little reflected light, the choice of ferns that grow successfully will be limited to those species native to these conditions. Others will not grow easily; fronds will be elongated and sparse and their colour a rather dull, and overall similar green. Fronds that colour in the autumn, and new spring growth that usually colours, will not be as pretty and the ferns will not be hardy enough to withstand any other hardships that come their way.

Micro-climate: An understanding of a garden's micro-climate is all important in planting. The patterns of light and air movement dictated by the position of buildings and trees will set up a climate within, and unique to, each garden space. Over the years this micro-climate can alter too. It may be changed suddenly by a neighbour's pulling down a building or felling a tree or the change may occur naturally as trees grow bigger, cast more shade and alter wind patterns. But, if you are aware of these things and the effect that they are having on plants, you can take steps to counteract changes.

Wind: Hot or cold, strong or sneaky, wind is one of a fern's worst enemies. In any extreme form it can distort and batter fronds, and retard new growth. So, if the aspect is good, ensure that it is protected from wind or provide that protection bearing in mind that the wind's velocity increases along a wall. A tree or a barrier of bushy shrubs should be sufficient to deter strong winds. Or a simple lath fence will do the job until shrubs grow in a new garden.

After a fern has been established for a while it will have aligned its fronds to prevailing winds, so if the natural or man-made protection is lost, and the direction of the wind changes, ferns can be severely damaged. Keep this in mind with building or tree-felling operations of any scale that are likely to alter wind direction or strength.

Soil

Good soil preparation is vital before planting. If the soil is not ideal for fern growing, it can be altered, but this soil conditioning then becomes a long-term project, and something that must be worked at regularly to maintain the desired condition.

Heavy soil: If the soil is a heavy loam it can be made quite suitable for fern growing with the addition of plenty of coarse and resilient organic matter, grit and gypsum (see page 31). These materials improve the aeration and prevent the soil from packing down and becoming hard again. A heavy texture is not a deterrent for fern growing as long as it is worked for a few months before planting, and leaf mould is applied regularly after planting — organic matter breaks down all the time and has to be replenished. The soil should be worked prior to planting to a depth of 24 to 40 cm (10 to 15 in) for small to medium ferns, and to a depth of about 60 cm (2 ft) for larger species like tree ferns.

Sandy soil: This can be made suitable for ferns if, again, plenty of organic matter in the form of peat moss and old manure is dug into it to help it retain moisture. Sandy soil is easy to work, and suitable for many ferns, especially the lime tolerant species and those that grow naturally among rocks. However, due to its lack of water retaining properties, it will need mulching well, watering deeply and frequently, and regular additions of humus.

Clay: It is a very long-term prospect to get clay into a condition suitable for fern growing, so it is usually best to dig it out and fill the pockets with top soil or imported soil. Good drainage may be necessary to ensure that the clay pan does not form a sump under the bed for ferns will not tolerate sodden conditions around their feet for very long.

Drainage

Good drainage is absolutely essential. After heavy rain watch the ground intended for a fern bed; if the water lies around for two or more days, the drainage is not good and must be attended to before planting. You can improve drainage by laying agricultural pipes or perforated plastic drain pipes under, and leading away from, the fern bed.

If drainage does become an insurmountable problem, an elevated bed could be the solution, using rocks and other drainage material laid under the soil. An alternative would be a rock garden to take ferns that are happy rooting in the cool protection of stones and grit.

Fertilisation

Immediately before planting new ferns, dig in a light dressing of bone dust. This readily available organic food will give the plants a good start in their new ground. No chemical fertilisers should be used at this stage—they can burn tender new root growth as fast as it forms.

Planning

Do plan ahead before putting new ferns into the ground. Plant so that individual ferns get a chance to show off a little and have a little territory to call their own, especially in their early years while they are still establishing. Big growing ferns like the *Polystichum, Dryopteris* and some of the *Athyrium* and *Todea* species will need at least 1 m² (1 yd²), and smaller species about 30 cm² (1 ft²). Creeping ferns will need about 1 m² (1 yd²).

It is tempting to overplant if impatient for something green and growing, but by doing so a great deal of the ferns' beauty of form and habit will be lost. It would be a pity not to be able to admire the perfect rhythm of a Blechnum's unfolding or the shapeliness of a bird's nest fern's nest part. Pity, too, to miss the fantastic other world of the embryonic fronds at soil level. There is nothing sadder than a glorious tree fern jammed into a corner where the great branching fronds cannot develop in their beautifully symmetrical way. They are big spreading fountain-like things that go up a little way each year, but out a long way in no time at all.

In the shade house

In a shade house, you begin to exercise some control over the elements, and can grow ferns that are normally not climatically suited to a particular area or garden. A shade house will cut down the amount of sunlight and create shade. It will affect temperatures somewhat (but not sufficiently in cool temperate areas to permit the growing of tender tropical plants). A shade house, in short, cuts down the exposure to extremes of anything, sunlight, temperature and wind, so that a much wider range of plants can be grown in these middle-of-the-road conditions. Sometimes ferns which are deciduous outside, keep their leaves all year round in the shade house, and often those that are merely frost tender in the garden and enter a semi-dormant period, keep growing and producing fronds through the winter months if kept in the shade house.

The shade house can be a very simple structure and a very flexible one. If made of brushwood, laths or shade cloth, the amount of shade required can be achieved by laying the laths or brushwood closer together or further apart, or selecting a shade cloth to give the percentage of shade suitable.

It can be left just a light structure with roofing only if shade is all that you need, or the sides can be filled in with the same materials to protect against prevailing winds. The humidity can be increased readily in the shade house by keeping the earth floor dampened, and in winter you can remove alternate laths or brush to allow more sunlight through.

Shade cloth can be bought in several densities, 32 per cent, 50 per cent, 70 per cent and 80 per cent being the standard materials. The higher the percentage, the denser the shade provided. The degree of shade required will be dictated by the aspect of the growing area and the proximity of overhanging trees or of nearby buildings—a white painted building can reflect a lot of light. In the Southern Hemisphere, a shade house with a north-west aspect will require a high percentage of protection. The same applies to a shade house in the Northern Hemisphere with a south-west aspect. If a deciduous tree shelters the shade house during the summer months, the degree of protection can be greatly reduced to say about 30 per cent filtering of light.

In the glasshouse

In a glasshouse, you can exercise almost complete control over light, temperature (if it is heated) and humidity, so that almost any fern can be cultivated.

However, the trouble with commercially made glasshouses and books about growing in glasshouses, is that they are oriented to the grower who wants hothouse and flowering plants. The houses are usually constructed to attract and make the most of maximum sunlight, and books about growing techniques will advise on how to plant the house with this in mind and grow the plants that enjoy these conditions. Ferns usually come as an afterthought when it is found that staging provides some shade underneath.

Adapting the Glasshouse for Ferns

An existing glasshouse, or a glasshouse built in an exposed position, can be made quite suitable for ferns if the roof and exposed sides are shaded. This can be done by the conventional white-washing method, but with another coat applied with a kind of stippled effect, so that the plants can enjoy dappled shade like that in their natural habitat. Lath blinds make a flexible, long-term, though rather expensive, shading. They can be rolled up in winter to allow more light through and should be hung so that the slats are running north-south. They will then cast shadows quickly as the sun climbs in the summer time. Blinds can be made, too, out of shade cloth, or scrim. To lengthen the life of these material blinds, make them so that they hang inside the roof, as long as the sun shining directly on the glass does not generate too much heat.

An ideal glasshouse for ferns is one that is shaded for most of the day, for most of the year. Often the side of a house is suitable

and can be an excellent location for a kind of lean-to structure. If there is a doorway or window that is not used often because the prospect from it is rather dreary, it may be opened onto a whole new world—of ferns. Glass-in the doorway and the little world will become part of the house. This kind of fernery attached to the house is much easier and more economical to heat.

Ventilation

Good ventilation is crucial to the successful management of a glasshouse. This way extremes of temperature and sudden rises and falls can be avoided. In a commercially made glasshouse adequate ventilation will be provided. In a do-it-yourself glasshouse ventilation must be planned very carefully into the structure, especially where artificial heating will not be used. Ventilation at the top is more essential than at the sides, for if the top vents are open heated air will be able to escape, and fresh air can find its way in even though vents may not be installed at the sides of the house. Small openings on each side of the roof ridge, or a hood ventilator extending the full length of the building are sufficient. To prevent down draughts and through currents of air, the vents on the lee side only need be opened.

Temperatures are best managed by admitting air early in the mornings and closing the vents early in the afternoons.

Ventilators too can be opened to prevent the temperature from rising too sharply and to let in fresh air and keep that air circulating; essential in summer as damp stagnant air encourages the growth of moulds and bacteria and equally important in winter as damp stagnant air encourages frost damage. Ventilators should only be closed completely if a gale, dust storm or fog is threatening—always keep at least one open on the leeward side of the house.

Frost

Frost in an unheated glasshouse can be prevented by lowering the sun blinds on the roof to conserve as much heat absorbed from the daylight hours as possible, and providing an effective barrier between the plants and the glass, such as newspapers or brown paper. It is a good precaution to cut right down on watering during frosty spells and to keep the atmosphere as dry as possible, and the air moving. If the ferns do freeze they will need very gradual thawing out of direct sunlight. Plants in pots should be lifted off the floor (always the coldest part of the house), and plunged into boxes or larger pots lined with paper, rags or straw—anything that will insulate the pot and the plants' roots against the cold and possible freezing.

Heating

A glasshouse can be heated by several means. A small boiler (gas, coke or oil-fired) and the necessary piping for the hot water circulation is an old but still very efficient method. The pipes maintain a uniform and evenly distributed temperature without hot and cold spots, and the upkeep, after the initial installation costs, is not high. Electrical heating is perhaps a little more modern and can be arranged through a coil system throughout the house or by heating the concrete floor slab. This gives a very even, but dry, heat and the dryness must be counteracted by humidifiers. Individual kerosene heaters placed at intervals throughout the house are perhaps the cheapest method of heating in terms of initial outlay and running costs, and the fumes do not pose a problem if the burners are efficient and the house well ventilated. Large individual gas burners that blow hot air around the plants are used in many commercial nurseries these days, but they must be strategically placed so that hot draughts do not dehydrate the foliage.

As a guide to temperatures within the glasshouse, the following is an internationally accepted scale: cool 7-15°C (45-60°F), intermediate 12-21°C (55-70°F), and warm 18-26°C (65-80°F). The minimum temperature at which tropical ferns are grown should be 12°C (55°F), but many subtropical species will thrive with a minimum temperature of 7-10°C (45-50°F). Excessive heat will only encourage premature growth which is very vulnerable to any hardship. But the most important aspect of heating a glasshouse is

that the temperature is kept constant, only varying by a few degrees, and that an even temperature is maintained within a range recommended for a particular fern. If for economical reasons the winter temperatures have to be kept slightly lower than those recommended, the fern will not necessarily die, but will probably enter a dormant stage and may shed its fronds.

Indoor growing

We ask much of ferns when we grow them inside a house, so there is much to do to make up for placing them in such strange circumstances. There they sit, their roots encased in an alien substance, tightly strictured within the hard walls of a container and totally dependent on some human's whim for food and water, with house dust, fly spray and cooking fumes wafting around them and adding to their misery. They may be desperate for cool damp air, but the human feels cold, or worse still, has gone away and the window is shut and the air is stifling. Even if the surroundings are congenial, there is always the likelihood that a fern will be whisked away, without warning or ceremony, to some other place less than congenial.

And yet a house should be a good place for ferns to grow, especially the tender ones that will not tolerate extremes of anything. The air in the house is usually much milder than outside; temperatures are less extreme and less prone to sudden changes; and the light is usually softly filtered through blinds or scrim curtains, even to the point of being gloomy like a fern's natural habitat, the forest. These ideal conditions evidently prevailed in houses in Victorian times and were probably the reason that ferns became so popular as house plants (they were, in fact, the first house plants). Another factor that made them easy to grow in those days was that the average house always had a kettle simmering on the hearth (or so one reads in books about growing ferns in Victorian times), which kept the atmosphere relatively moist—the key to successful indoor fern cultivation.

Humidity

The atmosphere inside the average house these days is just too dry for ferns. The only rooms where any degree of humidity is maintained are the kitchen, bathroom and laundry. The kitchen atmosphere is usually adulterated by cooking and fuel fumes, and in all cases the humidity is not a constant thing, as cooking and bathing are not constant activities. Still, they are probably the best places as long as the natural light is sufficient, the air circulates freely within that room and the temperature is constant. This does not mean that you must banish all your ferns to the bathroom or laundry, where you cannot see them all the time, because the humidity in any room can be increased and maintained at a fairly constant level quite easily.

Grouping: Grouping several ferns around a bowl of water is probably the most simple and a most effective method. Or group them on a tray or dish that contains water. Stand the individual pots on pebbles placed in the tray so that the plants are standing *over* the water, not *in* it. (Ferns should never touch or absorb the water on which they stand.) An inverted saucer standing in a deeper dish of water works well this way too.

Grouped plants protect each other and trap much needed humidity

Grouping plants adds to the effect of any humidifying methods that are employed. When several pots of ferns are grouped on a tray or over water, they afford some protection to each other and seem to generate their own micro-climate around themselves. All plants give off water vapour through their leaves in the transpiration process and the vapour creates humidity around each transpiring plant. A group of plants will create more humidity which they can all share. The increased moisture in the atmosphere will mean that the plants require less attention to their water needs, while the water tray beneath a lone plant always seems to need topping up, or the fronds need extra spraying to keep them looking fresh and happy.

Spraying: Another way of keeping the moisture content of the air fairly high is to spray around the plants with an atomiser, which you keep near the plants for that purpose. The water in the atomiser should be at room temperature. A discarded plastic bottle with a spray top is useful for this, or one of those excellent pressurised spray guns if there is a big area to maintain. Do not overly wet the foliage, just dampen the air immediately around it. This is a useful method to boost the humidity on an especially dry day.

The rate of evaporation will increase with the room temperature, creating a relatively high humidity, provided that there is protection from draughts which will disperse the vapour. But remember that the warmer the air, the faster the humidity in the air will be dispelled.

Watering

Watering indoor ferns is a matter of knowing the individual plant's needs and experiencing the plant's habits in a particular situation. A position close to a window, which gets a little morning sunlight, will cause the pot to dry out much more quickly than if the same potted plant is placed on a table a metre or so from the same window. Plants grouped over water will dry out much less quickly than one sitting by itself in the same size pot and in a dry saucer. When plants are grouped the rate of evaporation from the sides of a clay pot and the top soil is greatly reduced.

Potted plants dry out much more quickly inside a house than in a protected place outside. A reason for this is that the generally warmer temperatures inside the house speed up transpiration or moisture loss through the leaves. Also the relatively low humidity in the air of the house will draw water out of the soil in the pot. This will be good for the immediate air around the plant but it does deprive the roots of water.

Cutting down evaporation: The evaporation of water from the soil in the pot can be cut down by mulching the top soil with peat moss, sphagnum moss, leaf mould, paper, foil, anything that will ensure that the soil underneath stays damp. Another most effective method is to sink the pot or pots into a larger container lined with any of the above materials. It is then extra work to extract the pot and water it thoroughly but because this method does cut down evaporation so effectively, it just about halves the number of watering times. The pots can be hosed and flooded outside, drained thoroughly so that they are free from drips, and plunged back into their protective container.

Protecting furniture: The dampness underneath the pot of any house plant is always a problem because of the damage that it can cause to furniture and floor coverings. The most effective way of coping with this is first to ensure that the newly watered plant has drained completely, and then place it on a glazed saucer—an earthenware one will absorb moisture from the pot and leave water marks on the surface beneath. It is a good idea to make a buffer zone under any kind of saucer by lifting the saucer onto a wire or wood frame, which also helps the air to flow around the plant.

Hazards

Winter: Winter is the worst time for a fern growing indoors. Fluctuating temperatures and low light levels at this time of the year are the biggest problems. Indoor ferns can be thriving during the spring and summer when

the house is open and gentle breezes blow through, clearing away cooking fumes and tobacco smoke. In these seasons temperatures are fairly constant and the humidity level is maintained by the changing air.

In winter windows and doors are usually closed and individual rooms heated, often sporadically, so that temperatures fluctuate at an alarming rate for even the hardiest house plant. A typical situation is when a room is heated in the evening by a fire of some type and the fire is turned off when the household is ready to go to bed. The fern is left in a rapidly cooling room which by morning is downright chilly. During the next day the room may be warmed again by the sun, only to cool down again at sunset. Later in the evening the fire will be lit and the poor fern will have been subjected to something like four temperature changes in the space of twenty-four hours! Plants growing indoors, even if they are thriving at other times of the year, are just too soft for such traumas and will be set back each winter. They will pick up again in the spring if conditions are good, but the constant winter setback will take its toll on the look and growth of the plant.

Plants grown in centrally heated houses are slightly better off in the winter. At least the temperatures are constant, though the atmosphere is usually dry.

The generally lower light levels, and fewer actual light hours inside a house in the winter are big problems. Growth slows down in the winter because of the reduced number of daylight hours. In normal growing times the light inside a house is cut down, which suits a fern, but the number of light hours remains the same as those outside. In winter the number of daylight hours is often unwittingly cut down by the early drawing of blinds and curtains to retain the warmth. At the same time, reflected light that is often a useful energy source for indoor plants is cut down by the generally gloomier conditions. This combination of fewer daylight hours and reduction of light intensity can be very damaging.

If these conditions prevail in a house, the indoor ferns are better off outside for the winter, in a very sheltered, frost-free place, and being brought inside only occasionally for decoration. Outside they will, at least, get enough light for their needs, and even if it is cold they will adjust and enter a dormant period. In this way they will not suffer as much damage as they are likely to from fluctuating temperatures, low light levels and a dry atmosphere.

Windows: Temperatures can vary considerably immediately around a plant if it is kept close to a window. Glass conducts cold very easily and can be quite icy to the touch, so that the side of a plant near to the window can actually be burned by the cold, while the side away from the window is faring quite well. Keep the green parts away from direct contact with the glass, and provide some insulation, ideally a scrim curtain, between the pot and the glass too, as the roots can be traumatised by the intensified cold.

In fact, windows are hazardous places at any time. Temperatures in the vicinity can be degrees hotter or colder than the interior of the room. And draughts sneaking in under ill-fitting joinery and weather proofing can often be the least suspected, and most likely cause of a plant's growing poorly. Feel around cracks on cold blowy days—if there is a draught be assured that the fern has felt it already and some sort of adverse reaction has taken place.

Fumes: Fumes from cooking, smoking and sometimes from winter heating appliances can be the cause of poor growth. Gas and oil burning fires usually have enough built-in installations to ensure that fumes are removed so a plant is usually safe enough in a house heated this way as long as the humidity is maintained and the air circulates freely. Ferns seem to have a great deal of tolerance for kerosene fumes, for I know of several glasshouses that are heated in this way. It is really the direct heat from any form of heater that is most damaging, not the negligible fumes.

Light

A sunny aspect is one that faces east and where morning sun pours through the window, making the room warm and light.

This aspect usually means that the afternoon temperatures are cool and will be good for ferns as long as they are protected from late morning sunlight in summer. A westerly aspect, where the room gets the long rays of afternoon sunlight and where temperatures are usually high in the afternoon, is usually too hot, dry and bright for ferns.

In a room facing north in the Southern Hemisphere, south in the Northern Hemisphere, there is usually plenty of light, if not sunlight, for most of the day. This aspect is too bright for most ferns and they will need some protection. A room facing south, in the Southern Hemisphere, north in the Northern Hemisphere, which gets plenty of light but no direct sunlight, should be good for ferns as long as they get the maximum amount of light that comes into the room.

Altering light levels: The light levels, of course, can be altered. A sunny, north-facing room, or south-facing room in the Northern Hemisphere, planned to make the most of the aspect with light-painted walls and plenty of windows will be much too bright for ferns. Paint that same room dark green and cover the windows with bamboo blinds and it will probably be ideal. Light levels can be altered by the use of lightweight curtaining or blinds, or with an outside blind, or a tree or shrub planted outside the window (a deciduous one will make the seasonal adjustments). Over-hanging eaves and pergolas gently filter the light to suit ferns.

Low light levels usually apply to dark rooms, hallways and dark corners of otherwise light rooms. Few ferns can tolerate these conditions for any length of time and will need some form of artificial light, or frequent, to the point of daily, sojourns outside. If there is one strong direct light source in a room, the fern will tend to grow towards that. If you do not notice this in time the plant will develop a permanent lean in that direction as its tissues harden. Any new growth will come from the hardened part of the stem or frond which accounts for odd kinks in the fronds. This can be counteracted by turning the plant as frequently as every day, as growth is that constant.

Artificial light: If planning to use artificial light methods, set up a whole area or corner of a room and devote it to this kind of growing, because the light source should be directly above and close to the plants. The height of the lamps should be adjustable to allow for growth, so that the whole setup has to be very carefully planned. There are many ready-made units available, home assembly is easy once the principles of growing plants with artificial light are understood.

It is first important to understand how a plant uses light. Natural sunlight is composed of energy forms which are used by plants for growth, food and energy production, and germination and blooming. When growing plants away from natural light the light sources which most nearly duplicate the essential elements of the sun's rays should be substituted. These light sources are not uniform in their quality or quantity of radiant energy.

Special fluorescent tubes have been developed to simulate actual sunlight rays and are used to stimulate growth in all areas. But the plain fluorescent (white) light which is strong in the blue and violet areas of the spectrum can supply sufficient light needs for growth. (The blue and violet areas stimulate phototropism, which is growth towards the light, and photosynthesis, which is the manufacture of food.) They are also more satisfactory because they are cooler and less expensive than the specially developed tubes. The radiant energy of these tubes can be increased considerably without scorching plant tissues if a reflector of some description is used too. The plain fluorescent can be used successfully in conjunction with the less expensive incandescent bulbs. These bulbs should not be used alone as they are not strong enough in the red and blue colour bands, and they generate too much heat, which may scorch delicate fern growth. (The red colours in the spectrum stimulate photosynthesis and phytochrome — the plant material which causes germination and growth.)

A good general type of artificial light to use for ferns and other, what are called low energy foliage plants, is a cool or warm white light. A standard amount of light required for this type of plant is 15-20 watts of light per 930 cm² (1 ft²) of growing surface.

The lamps should be changed every one to one and a half years as their radiant energy decreases greatly with time, even though they still give out light. They should also be cleaned regularly to maintain efficiency for they attract dust by static electricity.

Another point to bear in mind when using artificial light for growing or stimulating growth, is that plants need both light and dark periods, so provision should be made for the lighting to be turned off at regular intervals to simulate night time conditions. Foliage plants, like ferns, need ten to twelve hours of light a day, and it is important that this schedule is regular to maintain healthy growth.

General Maintenance

If the conditions inside the house are even one fraction less than ideal, indoor ferns should be spelled outside from time to time. A few days outside in mild, windless weather will be a real tonic for house-bound plants, especially those that have been subjected to indoor winter hazards. As many outings as possible in gentle rain showers, at any time of the year, will do lots of good washing off house dust and rinsing salts out of the potting mix.

In order to harden them a little, ferns should be left outside for as long as possible, no matter how close to ideal the conditions are inside. But, choose the right time. Take them out very early in the morning so that they can adjust to the growing light gradually, and keep an eye out for any turn for the worse in the weather.

If the conditions inside the house are not good, try to keep the plants outside for at least three days at a time, and inside for two days at the most. If the potted plants are used just as decorative accents around the house and conditions are far from ideal, it is useful to have two plants for every spot that you want to decorate and alternate them, making sure that each is outside longer than it is inside.

FERNS IN CONTAINERS
7

Ferns are obliging container plants, demanding little of their keeper's time and energy. They are often content to stay in the same container for years, only asking to be repotted when their roots are overcrowded and growth becomes thin. And often they will go back into the same pot, which is great if that particular combination of plant and pot is pleasing.

Pots and potting

The success of growing ferns in pots depends initially on the choice of a suitable fern, careful potting, an efficient drainage system, an appropriate potting mixture and, above all, careful watering which will make or mar the whole.

Suitable Ferns

The choice of a suitable fern means confining pot cultivation to those species that are smaller and less strong growing. This does not mean that the others will not grow in a pot at all; it means that the bigger ones, and those that grow quickly, like *Nephrolepis cordifolia, Pteris cretica, Adiantum raddianum* and all tree fern species will have to be continually repotted in larger containers to maintain a healthy, steady growth, until eventually they become too big to be handled easily.

Suitable Pots

Any conventional plastic or clay pot, a hanging basket made of wire, plastic, clay, wood, bamboo or wicker (hanging baskets have a section to themselves, see page 67); old iron kettles and china chamber pots or tea pots, if their rustic or interesting character takes the fancy; old laundry troughs of timber or cement; discarded washing machines, barrels or coppers; those always-good-looking and suit-any-kind-of-plant half beer and wine barrels; tubs, big and small—anything that pleases, is an appropriate size, a good shape and which will complement the fern intended for it.

Any pot used should have a good size hole in the bottom, or a number of holes around the sides that will let excess water flow away easily. Sometimes the holes in a new terracotta pot have not been punched out sufficiently and will need a few extra pushes with a stick to clear them. A masonry drill can be used to improve the holes in a cement tub and a hot poker will do the job on plastic pots.

For pots without drainage holes, take extra care with initial potting to provide plenty of drainage material in the bottom, to water with pure rainwater only, and to ensure that the plant is not overwatered.

If ferns are kept outside in plastic pots, the temperature of the soil in the pot will be approximately the same as that of the surrounding air, because plastic does not have the insulating qualities of wood or clay. This is very relevant on a day of extreme temperatures, or if the pot is sitting directly on a masonry or metal surface, or is hard up against a surface that reflects heat and cold.

Catchpots or cover pots: These come in all shapes and sizes and do a good cover-up job on an otherwise ugly plastic or clay pot. They are usually sold with the explanation that they catch the drips—a point to be wary of. Catching the drips is fine, but the pot containing the roots must not be allowed to stand for any length of time in the accumulated drips or the soil will go sour. This can be avoided by standing the container pot on a layer of pebbles or an inverted saucer inside the catchpot.

More importantly, catchpots insulate the container and keep the roots at a more even temperature than if the pot is fully exposed. This keeps the growth rate steadier and the plant generally healthier. The insulation is made more effective if the space between the container and the catchpot is packed with one of the mulching materials like peat moss or paper.

Cement tubs: These are quite suited to fern culture. The small amount of lime used in their manufacture does not affect the soil chemistry. They are best left unpainted for they remain more porous that way, keeping the soil aerated. Their rather raw new look does mellow with time, so that the white and grey ones take on a rather nice old weathered look. Really big cement tubs should have extra holes bored through the base to allow for efficient drainage.

Pans: Wide shallow terracotta pots, often called "pans" by nurserymen, are ideal for fern growing.

Wooden tubs: Big wooden tubs and barrels intended for long-term use should be charred with a blow torch, or given a coat of bitumen paint to help preserve them. If the drainage hole looks inadequate for efficient drainage, extra holes should be bored in the tub's base.

Clay, wood and plastic pots: I always think that a plant breathes a sigh of relief when put into a clay or wooden pot, and though I concede many of the arguments put forward in favour of plastic pots, I am sure that clay and wood are closer to a fern's natural condition. However, to be more scientific, ferns do equally well in plastic, glazed, or clay pots, if the different qualities of each are understood and kept in mind.

Clay or wooden pots dry out much more quickly than plastic pots, but they do provide more aeration for the soil by nature of their porous sides. Because the aeration is better in a clay pot, a heavier soil mix can be used; whereas the soil mix in a plastic pot should be lighter and should drain more readily. The walls of a clay or wood pot will hold moisture too, so that there is extra moisture for the roots to use if necessary. However, salts and algae are more likely to build up in a clay or porous pot as they become trapped within the walls.

Plastic pots are, of course, very light and easily handled which makes them ideal for the commercial grower and those who go in for potted plants in a big way. They may not be such a long-term proposition as clay pots, for a certain amount of weathering (depending on the quality of the plastic) causes the material to break down—but then, a dropped clay pot is usually a broken pot!

Pots to avoid: Fern roots are on the whole wide and near to the surface, so that any depth of soil beneath the roots is not always

used quickly enough and can increase the risk of sourness building up. For this reason, deep pots are not the most suitable, though they can be suitably adapted with crocking.

Wooden containers made of treated pine are best avoided. Though most attractive with their soft green colouring, large amounts of chemicals are used in their weatherproofing. These chemicals can seep into the soil and upset its balance, often to the point of causing root and foliage burn.

Another unsuitable type is the "Ali Baba" shaped pot, where the neck is very much narrower than the body. It is almost impossible to get a plant out of a pot like this without awful damage to the root system or to the pot itself.

Those pots advertised as "self-watering" should be avoided. My objection to them is that the watering is not thorough enough, so that accumulating alkalies are not washed out of the pot. They also maintain a constant state of "wet side of moist" so that sourness can develop. They discourage, too, a "dry side of moist" condition in the soil which is necessary at regular intervals as a stimulant to root growth.

Cleaning pots: All pots should be thoroughly cleaned before use. This may sound overly careful, but it is a good precaution to take. As any experienced nurseryman will advise, "dirty pots only carry trouble".

Size and Preparation of Pots

The pot size will depend on the size of the fern. That is, the diameter of the pot should be about one-third the height of the fern, for ferns like to have their roots fairly snug about them. This is one of the reasons for a fern's thriving in the same pot for many years.

Old pots made of terracotta often look rather attractive with their sides encrusted with moss and salt, but these must go. A good soaking in mild, soapy water, a thorough scrubbing and a final rinsing in boiling or disinfected water is necessary, otherwise old pots will be an endless source of trouble with fungus and root diseases. Plastic pots should have the same treatment

—minus the boiling water. If salt crusts are stubborn, a little vinegar will dissolve them, but thoroughly rinse off after use.

Any wood or clay pot should be saturated before use so that it does not absorb any moisture from the soil and deprive the newly potted plant's roots.

Drainage

For a potted fern it is most important that the drainage system in the pot is in perfect working order for the duration of the fern's stay in that pot. Many people dismiss old-fashioned methods such as crocking as unnecessary nowadays, because some newly developed potting mixes, many of which are soil-less, are self-draining. This may be so, but my criticism of these mixes is that they remain too wet for too long. However, if they are used in a pot that pot will need good drainage and most careful watering, more so than with the conventional mix.

To construct an effective draining system in a conventional terracotta pot with a large hole in the bottom, first cover the hole with a piece of perforated zinc, galvanised wire (if the plant will not be in the pot very long) or fine plastic netting that will prevent worms, slugs and earwigs from collecting in the hole area. This may not be necessary for a few potted plants grown indoors, but is a good precaution if many potted plants are kept outside or in the greenhouse.

Over the wire goes a curved piece of broken crock, convex side upwards—the idea being to shed the excess water down underneath it and through the hole. If plenty of crock pieces are available, layer them over this key piece, all convex side up and even the space above them with gravel or pebbles that are free of dust. Make sure that the first, important piece of crock stays in place and that no small stones get into and block the drain hole.

A purist now puts in a layer of sphagnum moss, very coarse peat or fibrous material (in a big tub, a layer of grass turves, grass side down) over the drainage crocks. This is done in order to prevent fine soil particles washing down into the crocks and blocking up the carefully constructed drainage system.

A 15 cm (6 in) pot should have about 5 cm (2 in) of drainage material, and a 25 or 30 cm (10 or 12 in) pot about 8 cm (3 in). The tiny "thumb" pots used for newly propagated plants do not need crocking as the plant is not in them for very long. A big wooden or cement tub that is being prepared for long-term use should have at least 15 cm (6 in) of crocking and a very generous layer of turves, moss or fibre placed over it. If the pot is a particularly deep one, and unsuited to fern roots, the crocking should be increased accordingly.

Plastic pots which have holes all the way around the sides should be filled with coarse, but even-sized gravel chips to a height just above the top of the holes. Moss or fibre can then be layered over the gravel.

Potting Mixtures

There are many excellent ready-made proprietary brand mixes on the market which take the worry out of potting if you wish to grow just a few ferns in pots, indoors or out. Make sure that they contain soil, peat moss and sand in about equal quantities, and be aware that if they contain soil substitutes or synthetic matter like styrofoam, that regular fertilising and careful watering will be necessary. Some of the commercial mixes become waterlogged easily. If you find this happens, increase the drainage materials in the bottom of the pot, or water less frequently—but very thoroughly. Or you can adjust the mixture by adding more coarse sand. If the commercial mix seems to drain and dry out very quickly, add more water retaining material such as peat moss.

To make your own potting mixture, a good standard mix is: 1 part by volume of good loam, 1 part by volume of coarse sand, and 2 parts of well-rotted leaf mould. To each 4 buckets of this mixture add a 15 cm (6 in) pot of charcoal pieces, and a 2 cm (1 in) pot of John Innes Base Fertiliser—all thoroughly mixed together.

John Innes Base Fertiliser is a fertiliser made up as follows: 2 parts by weight of hoof and horn meal 3 mm grist (13 % N), 2 parts by weight of superphosphate of lime (18 % P) and 1 part by weight of sulphate of potash (48 % K).

The John Innes No 1 potting mixture, mixed in the ratio of 2 parts of John Innes to 1 of sphagnum peat is also a good soil mix for ferns. Charcoal pieces should also be added to this mixture to help keep it sweet.

The John Innes No 1 potting mixture is as follows: 7 parts by bulk of medium loam (sterilised and sifted through a 1 cm (3/8 in) sieve, 3 parts by bulk of horticultural grade peat moss and 2 parts by bulk of coarse sand. To each 4 buckets of this mix add 40 g (1½ oz) hoof and horn meal, 40 g (1½ oz) super-phosphate, 20 g (¾ oz) sulphate of potash and 20 g (¾ oz) of chalk.

Both the John Innes base and the potting mixture can be bought ready made if all this seems rather daunting. If made at home, it is important not to alter the amounts experimentally. It is possible, however, to follow the formulae without sterilising the loam. Sterilising can be done by steaming the soil or cooking it in an oven at 93 °C (200 °F) for half an hour. The smell is awful.

Osmunda fibre which is available in the United States and used as an orchid-growing medium makes an excellent fern compost if you can find it. Use it straight or instead of peat moss in a conventional potting mix. Used in strips as it is sometimes sold, it can be wound around the roots of a small plant and the whole wedged firmly into a pot.

Whichever mix you decide to use should be well balanced, moisture retentive, freely draining and evenly damp when put to use.

Planting

First make sure that the roots of the plant to be potted do not quite fill the pot, or if the plant is a young one, that the roots will only reach the sides of the pot by the end of the growing season.

Place some of the potting mixture on the drainage materials, judging it so that the fern will be in the centre of the pot and that the topsoil will be 1 to 2 cm (¾ to 1 in) below the rim of the pot. Hold the plant with one hand and, while rotating the pot, add handfuls of soil. Allow the soil to flow into the spaces between the roots, and gently firm it down between the roots with something

slender like a pencil. Fill to the top and firm the whole plant down by pushing gently around the base of the crown with your fingers. Give the pot a few firm taps on the side or tap the whole thing gently on a bench to settle the soil. The soil should still have some give in it, and the plant should be firm, and definitely without a wobble.

Gently and thoroughly water the new charge. Check after this watering that the pot is draining effectively; then put it in a sheltered place until it is looking happy. If the plant wilts and you are sure that there is plenty of moisture in the soil, spray around the green parts regularly until it picks up. A bell jar or a supported plastic bag placed over the pot and plant will help prevent dehydration. Do not be tempted to overwater at this stage, as the roots will not have recovered from the trauma of potting and will not yet be growing into the new soil, which can rapidly become sour.

Over-potting: Over-potting is one of the main causes of failure of potted ferns. The excess amount of soil holds too much moisture in proportion to the active roots and they cannot use up enough of it to keep the soil well aerated. The bacteria in the soil then die (drown), causing the sour odour. Growth stops and roots begin to rot, the top growth cannot support itself and that is the end of a favourite plant. The plant may indicate this condition by a perpetual wilt. If you suspect over-potting is the trouble, remove the plant from the pot and examine the soil and the root tips. If the soil is "gluggy", and the root tips brown and slimy, it should be repotted into fresh soil in a smaller pot, after the rotten parts of the roots have been trimmed. Thereafter water very carefully until growth picks up. If the plant still wilts, and the soil feels sufficiently moist, a spray around the foliage to keep the air around it moist might help. But it is hard to nurse a plant back to health after it has suffered a setback like this.

Repotting

Signs that a plant needs repotting are when growth is thin and poor in the middle of a pot, and any new growth seems to be coming mainly from around the outer edges of the clump: or when the clump has become densely matted and can no longer produce an even distribution of new healthy growth. A plant in such a condition needs frequent watering, its lower growth yellows and new fronds are stunted.

Two general rules that apply to repotting ferns are: first, they should be repotted only when the container becomes overcrowded and second, they should be repotted into a pot that is only one size larger than the one they came out of. Most ferns prefer to be slightly rootbound, with their stolons and creeping stems pressing against the sides of the pot.

The old soil mix should be thoroughly moist before the plant is taken out of the pot. If the plant is big, it is a good idea to soak it the day before and let it drain overnight. If it does not come out easily, run a long thin bladed knife around the pot between the soil and the sides, turn the pot upside down and, holding the plant at soil level between your fingers, gently tap the rim of the container on a wooden overhang like a shelf. The whole mass of roots, soil and crocks should come away as one and you can then gently untangle the outer roots. If it is difficult to scratch away the soil from such a mass, it is a good idea to roll the ball between your hand and a hard surface to loosen it. The plant is then repotted and firmed down in fresh potting mixture at the same depth as it was originally growing.

Increasing size: To increase the size of the fern to be repotted, trim off the dead parts and place it in a pot one size larger. If you wish to keep the plant in the same size pot, and it is a fern that can be divided—one that has several growing points—thin it to size by removing the smallest and weakest portions and any dead parts; then replace it in the pot with plenty of fresh potting mixture.

Dividing: If the plant is to be divided, remove it from the pot, and with a sharp knife, cut the clump cleanly into four equal sections. Where the centre growth is poor, cut this away along with any moribund parts, and place each section in a pot not much larger that itself.

For example, the four segments from a 15 cm (6 in) pot would each fit comfortably into a 10 cm (4 in) pot.

Three or four of these segments can be planted around a larger pot or basket, but this kind of growth is usually slow to establish and better specimens can be created by first planting into 8 to 10 cm (3 to 4 in) pots to grow for a while. Do not plant the segments deeper than they were originally, and firm them down well so that they are in close contact with the soil.

Some top growth should be cut back immediately a fern is divided, otherwise the foliage puts too heavy a demand on the depleted roots, and the plant can shrivel and die.

Routine Care

Routine care of potted ferns involves removing old fronds by cutting them off close to the soil level. This allows light and air to reach new growth and robs pests, like mealy bug and scale, of breeding grounds. Some ferns, like the maidenhairs, which become dormant or semi-dormant during the winter, can have all their fronds cut right back or burned off. This treatment is most effective in keeping down pests—it can be done by holding the pot and rotating it over a small fire so that remaining growth is charred.

Check that earthworms have not invaded the pots for their burrowing activity disturbs the roots. Small mounds of soil on the top soil and fine grains that collect in the saucers are a giveaway. Treasures that they are in the open garden, they are a real menace in a pot. They can be removed with a teaspoon and put into the garden, or the pot can be saturated in a weak solution of insecticide.

Moss and liverworts that grow on the soil surface should be removed, even though they can look quite pretty. There is an old theory that the state of the moss indicates the health of the fern, but they do deprive the roots of water and nourishment. This relationship may be workable in the ground, but I know of no study that has revealed its benefits for pot growing.

Aerating: Any pot is better for fern growing if

it is lifted off the ground slightly by means of a rack or pieces of wood, or bricks if the container is large. This allows for freer air circulation around the fronds, a freer flow of excess water from the drainage holes and better aeration of the soil mix within the container. It is also a good way to prolong the life of a wooden container, for it prevents the rot that often sets in from the bottom. A wooden barrel should be rested on the base boards, not on the staves, for its support, for these can be dislodged if they have to support too much weight.

Maintaining large potted ferns: A large plant in a large pot over any length of time is really only just going to get by, and will require a fair amount of work to maintain its growth and reasonable appearance. The best way to cope with such plants if repotting sounds like too big a task, is to scrape off the top soil each year and replace it with a super luxury mix of fresh potting mixture, bone meal and leaf mould.

Another method of maintaining some growth and a good appearance in a big potted plant, for example, a 1 to 1.5 m (4 to 5 ft) tree fern in half a 180 L (40 gal) capacity barrel, is to cut a channel a few centimetres inside the container wall, around, and completely down through the soil and roots with a long, very sharp knife. Working from the top, matted roots and any soil that are left in the channel can be removed from right around the root

A hose left trickling on top soil is an effective method of watering a large potted fern

ball. The remaining roots are then teased out and the edges replaced with fresh potting mix, leaf mould and bone meal. Though an effective method for getting some root stimulation to an old established plant, do not expect miracles. It will most likely only maintain growth and looks.

Watering is a problem with plants that have been in big pots for many years. They tend to wilt very easily for there is usually very little fibrous matter left in the soil to retain moisture—what soil there was has usually been washed away with time and a great mass of compacted roots tends to make up the sole contents of the pot. A hose left trickling gently on the top soil is probably the most effective method, combined with a good mulch to retain that moisture. Make sure that the water comes away from the drain hole steadily if you use this method; in a plant potted for a long time the roots will, more than likely, have clogged up the drainage system.

Terrariums and bottle gardens

Ferns have been growing in glass cases for more than one hundred years, though the elaborate Wardian cases of Victorian times have given way these days to simpler things like glass carboys, discarded fish aquariums and old glass-stoppered sweet jars. But together with hanging baskets, I suspect that terrarium-grown plants suffer the highest mortality rate of all growing things. They look lovely when first planted—intriguing little gardens of tiny plants, delightfully landscaped, and amusing and absorbing to plant and tend. They should stay that way as they are in an ideal climate of their own, sheltered, humid and protected from extremes of anything. Safe, too, from the devastation suffered by most indoor ferns from a dry atmosphere, tobacco smoke and fuel fumes and, above all, harsh handling of their delicate fronds.

Nothing should go wrong, but things do go wrong, horribly wrong. Awful black

Top: *Asplenium oblongifolium*
Bottom left: *Asplenium scolopendrium*
Bottom right: *Asplenium marinum*

Top left: *Athyrium filix-femina*
Top right: *Blechnum spicant*
Bottom: *Blechnum brasiliense*

Top: *Blechnum occidentale*
Bottom left: *Doodia aspera*
Bottom right: *Dennstaedtia davallioides*

Drynaria quercifolia, the oak fern

fungi take over and weird grey growths sprout on devastated fronds; thousands of nematode worms materialise out of the soil and wriggle up the sides of the bottle where they die and leave a nasty scum; unaccountable weeds thrive; strong growing plants take over and positively leap out of the top of the bottle and the whole thing becomes unsightly. What does go wrong is that they are watered too much and too often, or not at all when they need it; the soil is not sterilised; or the bottle is left standing in harsh or hot sunlight, so that the plants are burned. Often, too, the plants are too big when put into the bottle, and suffer awful root damage going through the hole. Or the wrong kind of plant is chosen —something like a potentially 1 m (4 ft) high *Polypodium*, which just loves the damp atmosphere and thrives to the detriment of everything else.

Choosing the Right Bottle

Any bottle will do, but bear in mind that no matter how big the bottle is, plants will outgrow it unless there is easy access to trim them regularly or replace them with something smaller. This is necessary because, if carefully maintained, the atmosphere is perfect for many ferns and they will grow well, so much so that sometimes within a few months of planting the bottle will be full of a dense green mass. If the hole is small, regard the garden as a short-term prospect, for if the plants do well, it will be impossible to get them out again without damaging their

Bottles with wide mouths are the easiest to maintain

roots. And if they are left in, they will soon fill the body of the container.

Preparing the "Bed"

As for any potted plant, there should be a layer of pebbles or scoria on the bottom of the bottle to allow for drainage. Any excess water will collect there, so the layer must be fairly deep. This way you will be able to see if too much water is accumulating, and the pebbles will keep the soil clear of any contact with it. Put the drainage material into a thoroughly cleaned and dried bottle. A thriving little garden through sparkling glass can look really pretty but if the bottle is left grimy, there will be a disappointing result. If the inner sides are left damp, fine dust particles from the potting mix may fly around the inside and adhere to the walls, spoiling the whole effect.

On top of the pebbles goes a layer of roughly crushed charcoal pieces—they can also be mixed in with the potting mix. This is necessary to keep the soil mix sweet and to some extent counteract any overwatering or lack of aeration in the soil.

An essential of the potting mixture is that it should be one which drains readily. Extra sand can be added to make it gritty, rather than extra peat moss which will make it moisture retentive. It is important that this mixture be sterilised to destroy any weed seeds or nematode worms, otherwise they will both take over. Sterilising can be done by baking the soil in a domestic oven at 93 °C (200 °F) for 30 minutes. The soil mix should be quite dry if it has to go through a tube to be put into the bottle. Dryness is not so important if the hole is large enough to get a hand right inside.

The easiest way to fill a small-holed bottle is to use a clear plastic tube (the plastic will bend so that it can be aimed where wanted) with a funnel in the top to stop the soil spilling down the outside of the tube and dirtying the bottle's interior. The depth of the soil will depend on the size of the bottle and the root size of the plants that you have chosen. If most of the plants are small, and one or two are big, you can compromise and make a mountain around the big ones, but overall, try to avoid too great a depth of soil in proportion to the size of the bottle, because it will look ugly.

The aim is then to get the soil evenly moist, not over-damp or muddy. Using distilled water, gently trickle it down the sides, or through the tube, aiming it where you think that it is needed most; or use an atomiser or an ironing bottle with a sprinkler top. This should be done very cautiously, even a tablespoon at a time if the bottle is small, and each measure allowed plenty of time to spread evenly through the mix. It is important not to hurry this part of the operation. If overwatered, and the soil looks "muddy", it is probably best to tip it all out and start again. If too much water accumulates in the pebbles in the bottom, and it is possible to get a hand through the opening, a bulb baster from a cookware shop might prove useful to suck it out again, or a long plastic tube used like a siphon.

Do not be tempted to leave what is obviously too much water in the soil in the hope that it will dry out in a few days, especially if the hole is small, because the idea is that the moisture is trapped within the bottle and drying out takes a long time! If the amount of water is not correct, sourness will build up quickly in the constantly wet soil, roots will rot and fungi and moulds will take over.

Planting

The smaller the plant the better; a large plant with a well-established root system will suffer a real setback if forced through the small opening of a bottle. Some nurseries will sell plants in tubes which are an ideal size (a tube is a seedling pot about 30 mm [1¼ in] in diameter). Sometimes it is difficult to obtain this size plant for most growers do not let their plants go at such an early stage in their development—it is not economical, and such baby plants are not hardy. If a local nurseryman can be persuaded to order some in, collect them as soon as possible and plant them immediately where they will be back in the same hothouse atmosphere and they will not be set back.

Be sure to check the plants carefully for pests and diseases before putting them into the bottle. Insects seem to thrive in the moist atmosphere and you may find that you are running an insect farm instead of a terrarium.

Getting a plant into the bottle takes much dexterity and patience. Lower it gently between two slender sticks or pieces of wire, or better still, by a length of black cotton tied around the root ball. The cotton can be used to pull the plant into position if the area is big and can be left there, where it will not be very obvious and will soon rot away. Firm the plant if possible, but it does not matter if it is a little loose for the roots will soon spread out and take a hold if conditions are good. Just make sure that the bottle is not moved too much or too roughly until all plants are growing steadily.

Maintenance

If the potting mix is thoroughly damp at the time of planting, the moisture can sometimes be sufficient for several weeks before any more water is needed. Watch the plants carefully for a few days, and only add water close to the roots if any of the plants shows signs of wilting. If one plant looks poorly and does not pick up, while the rest are looking good, it is probably best to assume that that one has suffered some root damage and should be removed.

It may take days to establish a correct moisture balance, which will be shown by the plants sitting up strongly and a dewy condensation on the upper sides of the bottle. This condensation may disappear off and on during the space of 24 hours; if it disappears altogether for a few days, as it may when the moisture in the soil mixture is getting low, watch closely for signs of wilting, and add water gradually until the moisture balance is established again. Moisture will evaporate more quickly if the hole is large and the bottle is not stoppered.

When the moisture balance is established, stopper the bottle. It need not be airtight, but it does not matter if it is. The idea is to establish a completely closed atmosphere which is virtually self sufficient for as long as possible—the plants will make their own micro-climate within the bottle. The moisture passed off from the leaves condenses on the sides and trickles down to the soil to be absorbed by the roots again. If the bottle is airtight the moisture will not have to be replaced for months on end.

However, if the bottle is airtight, you will have to watch that the level of carbon dioxide in the air does not fall too low. Plants use carbon dioxide during the day in the food-making process, photosynthesis, and exhale this gas at night during transpiration; the amount exhaled is never as much as that used during the day, so the amount in the atmosphere gradually diminishes. In a completely enclosed bottle, the diminishing level is accelerated by the fact that the bigger the plants grow, the more gas they use. This will be evident, for plants which until this stage have been growing well become weak and subject to fungous attack. Remove the stopper and let the gases rearrange themselves.

Keep the bottle in a place which gets plenty of natural light, especially if it is made of dense or coloured glass that may cut down the vital red, blue and violet colours of the spectrum. Keep it out of direct sunlight that may burn the foliage, and if the source of light is narrow and strong, turn the bottle frequently so that the plants will not develop a lean.

Fertilisation is not necessary. The plants will grow too big, too quickly.

Maintenance does not involve much work if the garden is thoughtfully and carefully planted. If you have mixed ferns with other indoor-tolerating plants, you may find that they lose the battle for root space if the atmosphere in the terrarium is conducive to other plants' good growth, for their roots are not competitive. An African violet makes a good companion, but as with all flowering plants in a terrarium, remove any dead flowers otherwise they may encourage the growth of fungi. Dead fronds should also be removed, and any strong growing plants that are threatening to take over. Keep a close watch at soil level and you may see, if the atmosphere is suitably moist, the delightful

beginnings of a new fern—the prothallus and a young sporophyte.

Suitable Plants

For a very small bottle or terrarium, say about 15 cm (6 in) in diameter, it is probably best to use the Selaginellas and the mosses. Some of the smaller Selaginellas are: *Selaginella brisbanensis*, *S. gracillima*, *S. australiensis*, and *S. apus*.

For larger containers suitable ferns to grow are: *Adiantum capillus-veneris* (southern maidenhair), *A. hispidulum* (rough maidenhair) and *A. raddianum* (delta maidenhair). *A. aethiopicum* (common maidenhair) would be suitable in a very large terrarium. The cultivars cv. Gracillimum, cv. Pacific Maid and cv. Pacotti, are also suitable. Others suitable for container growing include:

Anogramma—any of this genus of tiny short-lived ferns.

Asplenium flabellifolium (necklace fern) and many others of this species, *A. trichomanes* in particular (the maiden spleenwort).

Blechnum penna-marina.

Cystopteris fragilis and *C. filix-fragilis* (brittle bladder ferns).

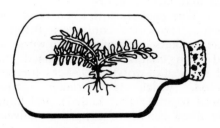

A new life for an old wine flagon

Doodia (rasp ferns)—many of this genus are dwarf growing. *Doodia caudata* is particularly suitable.

Hymenophyllum (filmy ferns). These ferns enjoy the high humidity in an enclosed bottle.

Mecodium demissum—a small filmy fern that enjoys high humidity.

Nephrolepis exaltata (Boston fern). The dwarf cultivars cv. Childsii and cv. Mini-ruffles enjoy being in a bottle.

Polypodium vacciniifolium.

Pteris (brake ferns)—the smaller cultivar cv. Wilsonii and varietas var. *albo-lineata* are suited to terrarium growing.

Ferns in hanging baskets

There are plenty of plants that look good and grow well in hanging baskets, and ferns do especially well because many of them are epiphytes and enjoy the light, airy conditions.

Any kind of container can be planted with ferns and called a hanging basket, but a container that is designed for the job will make the fern's life a lot easier. Something as simple as a terracotta pot slung in a fancy macramé bag will look good and do the job well, but the operation involved in getting a well established spreading fern out of the string and fancy work when it comes to repotting and tending time, will take a lot of patience and is bound to end up with broken fronds and short tempers.

Wire baskets with a generous amount of lining; terracotta containers fitted with chains; baskets made of tree fern wood, again fitted with chains and galvanised, firmly fixed supports; wooden baskets (preferably redwood, which is virtually rot-proof) screwed together (not nailed), and hung by firmly fixed chains of copper or galvanised wire, look good and are long-term prospects. They will not disappoint you by falling apart after a few waterings, hanging off centre, or proving impossible to replant without major renovations.

Strongly made wire baskets, of thick gauge wire that will not buckle and spaced so that the horizontal supports are not too far apart, are probably the most versatile. They are simple and relatively cheap to make up and hang; because of their unobtrusive feel, they combine well with all ferns and most other plants, and do not detract from the plants' form and colour.

The success of these wire baskets depends largely on the lining material. It must be lavish if the basket is going to last a few years, look attractive and do its job efficiently in all that time.

Sphagnum moss and paperbark linings are pleasingly natural and readily available from nurseries and plant shops. (It is illegal to take either of these materials from their natural habitat as well as detrimental to the environment.)

Moss should be used so that it is at least 8 cm (3 in) thick, and if it is kept moist, it may continue to grow, forming a dense mass, and look an attractive bright green. Paperbark is much easier to handle if it is thoroughly wetted and softened (hot water works most effectively) before it is used. It allows more room for soil mix and roots as it does not have to be used as thickly as moss. Both these materials are obliging in that they can have holes poked in them and creeping ferns and small Selaginellas can be planted in the sides of the basket. Several plants can be grown around the sides of the basket this way—peg them in with wire or secure them with extra handfuls of moss until their roots have taken hold. Ferns like *Nephrolepis* will soon discover any cracks in bark linings or chinks in the moss and pop out through them too.

The combination of the above two linings is effective. Put bark around the sides and moss in the bottom—the soil will drain easily through the moss; or bark underneath and handfuls of moss forming a decorative edging and useful mulch on top of the soil mix.

Moss and bark can be quite expensive if a lot of baskets have to be made. There are several equally efficient and much cheaper substitutes. These linings can be made to

The versatile wire basket carefully lined makes an ideal home for a fern

look prettier if they are covered with a thin layer of bark or sphagnum moss. Old and new carpet underfelt makes an excellent lining — use it lavishly with plenty of overlap because it does tend to shrink and compact. Canvas, denim, sacking or several layers of hessian also work very well, and can look good prettied up with a layer of moss between them and the wires. If several layers of material are used they will last several years before rotting away.

Natural materials, such as slabs of tree fern bark and coconut fibre make good long-term linings — they are slower to break down than sphagnum moss and paperbark. Fine wire and plastic mesh make excellent long-term linings, but need to be camouflaged with natural material for plants to look attractive. The fibrous sheaths that form around palm tree trunks are also an effective lining material.

Loose materials such as straw, spent pea plants, wood shavings and seaweed make cheap linings, but need to be backed with mesh or plastic sheeting otherwise they continually shed their particles.

In fact, it is a good idea to run a strip of plastic around the inside of the lining with any of the previously mentioned materials — it is a moisture saving compromise, and does protect the root systems a little from exposure to extremes of hot and cold. If plastic alone is used as a lining, use a green or black opaque, heavy duty plastic, not a clear one, for this will let light into the roots. Holes must be poked through the bottom so that the water will drain off.

Ready-made plastic pots with a built-in saucer and chain attachment make effective hanging baskets. Be sure to use a very open light potting mixture that drains readily and does not compact, especially if the fern is an epiphyte, and regularly tip out the accumulated drain water in the saucer. The drip catching saucer may be ideal for protecting the furniture and floor coverings, but it is a positive danger to the plant if water is allowed to stay in it for too long.

Baskets made of wood come in all shapes and sizes, and must be, as stressed before, very stoutly made if they are to be used as long term containers. The timber should be hardwood (which makes them heavy) and all the joints should be screwed together. The hanging supports should be made of galvanised metal or copper where they join the wood. Rope and twine supports quickly rot through if they are in contact with the soil, and are incapable of holding the sometimes very weighty mass of container, soil and plants.

Baskets made of hollowed out tree fern sections are almost ideal, though they will not last indefinitely for the wood is soft and rots easily. They are light and porous, capable of retaining moisture and yet permitting aeration of the soil within. Their fibrous quality makes them ideal for epiphyte ferns and those with creeping rhizomes for their roots can quickly penetrate, and take shelter and nourishment where they touch.

Ceramic pots are good for grounded ferns, but not for hanging ferns, unless they hang in sheltered positions and watering is regular and thorough. They dry out very quickly — even a cold wind can dehydrate the contents of a ceramic pot in a few hours. But they come in such a good range of shapes and sizes that they are hard to resist, in which case, there should be some means by which they can be taken down and soaked frequently and a heavier, moisture retentive potting mixture should be used. This will not suit epiphytic ferns, so stick to terrestrial ferns for these kinds of containers. Terracotta garden pots can be sunk into moss- or fibre-lined wire baskets and changed about frequently to suit your mood or the decor, but a word of warning about clay pots — they can be heavy, and very heavy when wet, so their supports should be sturdy.

One kind of ceramic pot that is particularly suited to epiphyte ferns is the one designed for orchids (many of which are epiphytes too). They are usually made of unglazed terracotta and are wide and shallow with large holes in the sides. Filled with gravel and a coarse open potting mixture, they are ideal for airborne ferns which love to pop out of the holes and scramble all over the sides. But, again a warning, watering must not be neglected because the orchid pots dry out easily.

The same soil mixtures and planting methods for potted ferns apply to basket ferns — a coarse open mix for epiphyte ferns and an ordinary potting mix for terrestrial ferns. Press the soil mixture firmly into place leaving at least 2 to 4 cm (1 to 2 in) below the rim of the basket so that there is room for a mulch and thorough watering. A mulch is a good idea as it will help cut down evaporation in exposed positions.

Old basket plants can be repotted when growth becomes thin and weak, or if the basket rots or breaks away. If the fern is still growing strongly and the basket has come away, it is often a good idea to sacrifice the basket and cut or break it away without disturbing the fern's roots and slip the whole plant into a slightly bigger, freshly lined container. If growth has thinned in the centre of an established hanging plant, try the rejuvenating technique of cutting out the dead centre portions, roots and all, and filling the hole with fresh potting mixture and leaf mould.

Most small growing ferns are suitable for baskets — epiphytes especially so, as they tolerate lower humidity. Terrestrial ferns often dry out too quickly or their fronds suffer low humidity damage, particularly if they are growing indoors. Pendulous and creeping ferns are particularly suitable as a hanging basket shows off their graceful habit to perfection.

Combinations are fun to get together.

The tall arching Polypodiums, the pendulous fishbones, and the delicate drapery of the soft feathery Lycopodiums look good. Long trails of small-leaf ivies tumbling out from among the fern fronds look good too, as do the asparagus ferns (not a true fern, despite its common name). Both do well in ferny conditions, but are inclined to take over fern territory, so be prepared for a battle if they are planted together. The variegated *Chlorophytum* or ribbon plant, with its quaint little plantlets on the end of old flower stalks, looks good among ferns — its cream and gold brightens an otherwise too green basket — but again, it is a strong growing plant and may need root pruning to keep it under control.

Baskets of flowering plants and ferns always look pretty, like giant bouquets, but there are few flowering plants that will continue to bloom in low light levels, the flowers becoming smaller and fewer. A couple of florist-forced *Polyanthus* among basket ferns in the spring time look pretty — they will enjoy the moisture and tolerate the gloom for a few weeks, but after that, they are best lifted out and placed in the garden, in semi-shade, where they belong. Orchids, on the other hand, may do well with epiphytic ferns. Their roots are not demanding and the naturally high growing epiphytic ferns will tolerate the filtered sunlight that orchids need during flowering.

A SELECT LIST OF FERNS
8

The following list contains almost 200 of the estimated 10,000 fern species in the world. They are, with few exceptions, ferns that anyone can grow in a house, in a garden, in a glasshouse, bushhouse or on a protected balcony or windowsill. Some may have special requirements such as a certain degree of heat in the winter; if so that is stated in the text. They are ferns that are readily available in commercial nurseries, through specialised growers or through the buying and selling of spores and plants among fern society members.

Only a few of the ferns listed are rare or rarely grown, and for these, botanical descriptions and any known cultivation notes have been included because they are mentioned in earlier chapters as being historically or botanically interesting or have been used as food, medicines or other saleable commodities. Ferns that are well known because of their attractive form have been included even if they require growing conditions that the average gardener may not be able to meet. This has been done so that the list is as comprehensive as possible and can be used as a reference for well-known and popular ferns throughout the world.

The main list contains terrestrial, epiphytic and lithophytic ferns. Tree ferns, aquatic ferns, filmy ferns and the fern allies and masqueraders are listed separately. Confusing botanical names and synonyms have been cross referenced. Common names have been included after the scientific name along with the name of the country where they are used.

The lists are arranged alphabetically by the scientific name, that is, genus and species, then any cultivars, varieties, subspecies or forms. The use of this terminology is universal and determined by standards set down by the International Rules of Botanical Nomenclature, which give each plant one name and one name only, and that name can be understood by everyone in the world. From time to time the discovery of new facts about a particular plant's structure or reproductive method has meant changes in its scientific name, and it has been moved from genus to genus according to the latest botanical theory. *Asplenium scolopendrium*, the hart's-tongue fern, is one that has been around somewhat. In such a case, it has been noted in the text and cross referenced, thus lessening the confusion and bringing the reader up to date with the latest terminology.

Individual species may vary. The variations can be to do with the spore bearing parts or frond structure, and may be due to hereditary or environmental factors, or may have been cultivated in the plant by growers. These differences within a species are labelled "cultivar", "forma" and "varietas". A cultivar (cv.) is a plant that has been "improved" under cultivation. A forma is so called when the changes have occurred in the natural environment and have remained constant through several generations. *Athryium filix-femina*, the lady fern, because of its genetic instability, is an example of a species that has given rise to hundreds of "forma" in its natural habitat. When changes have occurred naturally in the same species growing in different geographical areas the species are classed as varietas (var.) Subspecies (subsp.) is a term used in much the same way as varietas. Any changes are only noted by botanists if they are stable and have occurred in several generations.

Terms Used in Botanical and Cultural Notes

A small growing fern is one that is less than 30 cm (1 ft) high, a medium fern is one that is between 30 and 90 cm (1 and 3 ft) high and a large one grows to over 1m (3 ft). A large plant usually has the equivalent amount of spread and this should be allowed for in the planning and planting space.

A deciduous fern is one that drops all its leaves even in warm temperate climates. An evergreen fern is one that retains its leaves throughout the winter even if conditions are freezing.

Ferns in the list are referred to as hardy, semi-tender and tender. A hardy plant is one that will withstand long periods of freezing temperatures—these are plants from the cool temperate parts of the world. Semi-tender ferns are from subtropical areas and will not stand frost or temperatures below 15°C (60°F) at night. Tender ferns are those that need indoor or glasshouse protection, and extra warmth in cool temperate areas, so that the temperature in the growing area does not fall below 15°C (60°F) at night and 18°C (65°F) during the day.

ADIANTUM
(maidenhair ferns)

A genus of mostly terrestrial and small to medium growing ferns. All but a few of the 200 or so species have the classic shivering fronds that billow in soft clouds from a well grown plant, and the incredibly slender, dark stalks from which they take their name.

The common characteristic of the genus is the separate leaf stalk on all the pinnae or leaflets. It is these remarkably fine filaments that give the fronds the "floating on air" look. Even the comparatively heavy leaflets of the varieties like *Adiantum peruvianum* are supported on these amazingly strong, but delicate filaments.

Adiantum peruvianum (p.74)

Unfortunately they are not the easiest ferns to cultivate for they must have high humidity in the air around them. They are hardy in many respects, but can be devastated in a matter of days if placed in the dry atmosphere of an average house.

They are, too, strong growing plants that are happiest in a place in the garden or in a pot that fits their roots snugly, but being in that confined space they need regular feeding to maintain luxuriant growth. The soil for a potted maidenhair should be kept on the dry side of moist so that it is well aerated and the roots are constantly stimulated to seek water. The potting mixture should be on the gritty side with coarse fibre mixed through it to assist the drainage and aeration. Most species do well in soil that contains some limestone component such as marble chips, bone meal, oyster shell and agricultural lime. (At the New York Botanical Gardens maidenhair ferns are fed a twice yearly application of a lime in water suspension. They have to be divided twice a year.) Simply add 1 to 2 teaspoons of agricultural lime to a bucket of water and water each plant thoroughly.

In temperate areas growth in many species slows down in autumn and by winter the fronds have died back. This growth should be left in place where the climate is cold to protect the main body of the plant, and cut off just before spring growth appears; if left on the plant after the spring growing stage, it excludes light and air, and sometimes distorts new fronds. Watering must be cut down during the dormant period to prevent the rhizomes from rotting.

The centre of a plant that has been in a pot for a few years may die if the feeding has not been regular, and if the roots and old fronds have become matted. New growth can be stimulated by repotting, or by simply cutting out the dead centre portion, roots and all, and filling the hole with a luxury potting mixture rich in leaf mould. If by some mischance a plant shrivels completely because the soil dries out or the atmosphere is too dry, do not despair and throw the sad thing away — maidenhair ferns are fairly resilient and often come good again. Cut off the dead fronds, water thoroughly and watch for new croziers pushing up through the stubble growth. It may take some time before the plant is its luxurious self again, but at least it will still be alive.

Adiantum aethiopicum (common maidenhair). One of the best known and widespread Australian native ferns with a slender reddish-brown stipe arising from a closely growing rhizome. The pinnules are delicate and wedge shaped. Very easy to grow and quite vigorous, it will quickly outgrow a pot. It grows best in a semi-protected position in the ground in an area that is not totally shaded.

rather uncommon. It makes a quite hardy house plant, tolerating low light conditions as long as the atmosphere is not too dry and the soil is kept moist.

Close up of pinnules of *A. capillus-veneris*

A. capillus-veneris **cv. Imbricatum** (green petticoats). A popular cultivar that is rather difficult to grow. It likes a low to medium intensity light, a basic soil condition or potting mix and to be kept moist.

Left *Adiantum capillus-veneris*, right *Adiantum aethiopicum*

A. capillus-veneris (southern maidenhair, Venus' hair). Known commercially as *A. chilense* in the United States, this is a species widespread throughout the world, though now rare in Great Britain and found only in coastal areas in the south-west. In Australia it is found in the tropical areas growing in rock crevices close to water, but is again

A. capillus-veneris cv. Imbricatum

A. diaphanum (filmy maidenhair). Native to Australia, New Zealand, Asia and Polynesia, this is a delicate looking but easily grown fern. It has small, usually unforked fronds and distinguishing black hairs on the pinnules. It tolerates low to medium intensity light and does well in pots if kept moist. Will grow in extensive patches in sheltered situations.

Adiantum diaphanum

A. formosum (giant maidenhair, Australian maidenhair or black stem maidenhair). Found in Queensland, New South Wales, Victoria and New Zealand, this large growing and vigorous species is easily grown and suits open garden situations or a large pot.

Adiantum formosum

A. hispidulum (rough maidenhair, rosy maidenhair or five-finger Jack). Native to Australia, New Zealand, Asia and Africa, this fern is easy to grow. It is well suited to a rock garden or hanging basket. The new fronds are a delicate pinkish bronze.

A. pedatum (American maidenhair, five-finger fern). A dainty and distinct species native to North America, this is a small growing, hardy fern with palm-like, pea-green pinnules. It will tolerate deep shade.

Adiantum pedatum

A. peruvianum (silver dollar). One of the largest and most beautiful species, this is a unique maidenhair with its broad, oval-triangular blades which mature from pink to metallic green. The fronds may reach 1 m (3 ft) in length. It is rather tender and must have warm, moist conditions.

A. raddianum (delta maidenhair—also known as *A. cuneatum* and *A. decorum*). A semitender, rapidly growing small to medium size plant with filmy pea-green fronds. Native to central America, it requires high humidity, particularly if grown indoors. It is tolerant of shade.

A. raddianum cv. **Fritz Luth**. This fern is readily available and is characterised by its steel blue, shingled pinnules. It is an excellent house plant if kept moist but is semi-tender and requires protection if grown outside.

Adiantum raddianum cv. Fritz Luth

A. raddianum cv. **Micropinnulum** (baby's tears). Like many other plants with tiny leaflets it looks quite diaphanous and shimmering and, of course, is very popular. Unfortunately it is rather difficult to grow as it is semi-tender and requires a high humidity.

A. raddianum cv. **Pacific Maid**. A compact, small growing plant with a good contrast of colour between new and old growth, the new pinnules being a bright yellow-green. It makes a good house plant tolerating low to medium light conditions.

A. raddianum cv. **Variegatum**. As its name suggests, this cultivar is variegated, the frond tips having a number of white stripes. The wide fronds of this species are upright to pendent and thus it makes an attractive basket plant, though a large basket will be necessary.

A. reniforme. Originally from the Canary Islands where it flourishes in limestone crevices, this is a small growing unusual plant with large, kidney shaped pinnules on delicate but deceptively strong looking stalks. It is difficult to grow needing warmth and high humidity.

Adiantum reniforme

A. tenerum (brittle maidenhair). A small to medium growing, tender species from the American tropics. Tolerant of low light conditions and must be kept moist.

A. tenerum cv. **Farleyense**. A cultivar that has been much admired since its discovery in Barbados in 1865 when it was called "Queen of the Maidenhairs". A combination of rosy coloured new growth and light green old growth make this a very pretty plant. Like the species it is tender and rather difficult to grow needing glasshouse conditions.

Adiantum tenerum cv. Farleyense

A. tenerum cv. **Wrightii.** A trade named plant in the United States that is not registered. It is a choice house plant and looks good on an elevated pedestal or hanging basket as the fronds droop considerably.

A. trapeziforme (diamond maidenhair). One of the biggest species of the genus, this is an unusual maidenhair with large, diamond shaped pinnules borne on arching fronds. It is tender and requires glass or greenhouse conditions and extra humidity indoors to duplicate the tropical conditions of its original habitat in tropical America.

Adiantum trapeziforme

A. venustum. A hardy species reputed to come from Canada. It is a small growing plant with a blueish look to the mature fronds and makes a good addition to a rock garden.

AGLAOMORPHA

A genus of about 10 species of large, coarse epiphytes which form spreading crowns of foliage. In their native areas of Sumatra, New Guinea, Malaya and India they grow on trees and rocks. They are not commonly cultivated.

Aglaomorpha goeringianum pictum (Japanese painted fern—also known as *A. niponium* cv. Pictum). This is a colourful, hardy fern. The long, 60 cm (24in) fronds are an attractive combination of wine red with a central band of grey-green merging to green at the margin. Easy to grow and very hardy.

A. heraclea (also known as *Polypodium heracleum*). A tender species that needs plenty of light, high humidity, just moist soil, and good drainage, as well as protection from direct sunlight and frost. The base of each frond has the shield-like look of the Platyceriums. This species is suitable for a large pot or basket.

A. pycnocarpon (glade fern, narrow-leaved spleenwort). A slender, graceful fern from the North American woodlands. The fronds grow in almost circular clusters. It is deciduous and considered very hardy in the ground or in a pot.

A. thelypteroides (silver glade fern or silvery spleenwort). This is a very distinctive strong growing and hardy fern from North America. The common names come from the silvery indusia. It is further distinguished by the underside of the fronds which are covered in pale yellow hairs.

ANGIOPTERIS
(primitive ferns)

This is a genus of about 100 very primitive ferns some fossil remains of which have been found in rocks of the late Palaeozoic age. They are massive, easily grown plants and make a wonderful garden feature if they are given plenty of room to develop.

Angiopteris evecta (king fern or giant fern). A giant and primitive member of the fern family that is native to Malaysia and the northern parts of Australia's east coast. The fronds are reputed to be the largest in the world and have a strange, fleshy, unfern-like look. The plant is hardy and easy to grow, but must have plenty of room to show off its majestic self to full advantage.

Angiopteris evecta

ARACHNIODES

A genus of 50 or so medium sized terrestrial species which are found in South-East Asia, the Americas and Africa. The fronds, divided into three or four pinnae, are shiny with a harsh feel and have sharply pointed pinnules.

Arachniodes aristata (prickly shield fern). The only species of *Arachniodes* that extends to Australia. It is an easily cultivated if somewhat slow growing fern with a handsome look but harsh and prickly feel. It colonises creek edges by means of its long, creeping rhizome and if cultivated in the garden should be given some protection from sun and wind.

Arachniodes aristata variegatum

A. aristata variegatum. A hardy fern from Japan which is commonly cultivated in Great Britain. It has a yellowish variegation running up the centre of each frond.

ASPLENIUM
(spleenworts)

A mixed genus of ferns producing something as simple and as stylised as a bird's nest fern and as complicated and as exuberant as a mother fern. The genus is large, consisting of some 650 or so species

Asplenium adiantum-nigrum

distributed throughout the world, and containing both epiphytic and terrestrial ferns. There are many hardy species for cultivation.

They make excellent potted plants and are hardy inside the house if the humidity is fairly high and constant. Normal, well-balanced potting mixture is suitable for container growing, even for the epiphyte species. The epiphytes also lend themselves very well to basket culture.

The spleenworts that carry bulbils can be propagated easily from these baby plants. (See Propagation and Hybridising, page 42.)

Asplenium adiantum-nigrum (black spleenwort). Found throughout Europe, Asia, Africa, Hawaii and North America. The common name comes from the black colour of the stems below the rachis. It is a small growing, hardy plant needing medium light and moist conditions with perfect drainage.

A. attenuatum. An easily grown, hardy, but variable Australian species with long, gracefully pointed fronds which form masses of plantlets on the tips. Although very slow growing it is hardy and makes a good pot plant.

Asplenium attenuatum

A. billottii. See *A. lanceolatum*.

A. bulbiferum (mother fern, hen and chickens fern, mother spleenwort). Found in eastern Australia, New Zealand and Asia this is a common and easily grown house or garden plant which is tolerant of a shady spot. Like a giant carrot top the fronds grow to about 1 metre in length and cover themselves continuously with miniature reproductions of the parent plant. As they droop gracefully under the accumulated weight of baby plantlets they make an excellent basket or pot plant although a mature plant will need a garden position.

A. ceterach. See *Ceterach officinarum*.

A. daucifolium (Mauritius spleenwort—also known as *A. viviparum*). A small growing fern

similar to the *A. bulbiferum*, but in this case the plantlets have teardrop shaped leaflets with fine scalloping around the edges, giving the plant a peculiar grace. It is considered an easily grown plant for indoors, the glasshouse or fern garden.

A. falcatum (sickle spleenwort). Found originally in Australia, New Zealand, Papua New Guinea and Asia but now widely grown throughout the world. In its natural habitat it usually grows as an epiphyte on fallen tree fern trunks and in the pads of established staghorn and elkhorn ferns. Because of its epiphytic habit and long, mostly pendulous fronds, it grows well and looks good in a basket.

A. flabellifolium (necklace fern). From Australia and New Zealand, this species has long, narrow fronds and widely separated pinnae giving it the distinctive appearance from which it gets its common name. It colonises the rocky places where it grows by forming new plants at the tips of the fronds. It is a weak, but easily grown, plant for a pot, basket or sheltered position in the garden.

A. flaccidum (hanging spleenwort, weeping spleenwort—also known as *A. mayi* and *A. majus* in the trade in the United States). From Australia, New Zealand and some Pacific islands this is a variable species, mostly with narrow, pendulous fronds, often finely dissected so that it has a dainty appearance.

Asplenium fontanum

It is easily grown in a pot and also makes an attractive subject for a hanging basket.

A. fontanum (smooth rock spleenwort). A dwarf, hardy, tufted fern from central and southern mountain areas of Europe. The narrow fronds are dark green on top and pale green underneath. It grows well in a rock garden or small pot with a gritty potting mixture.

Asplenium marinum

Asplenium lanceolatum

A. lanceolatum (lanceolate spleenwort — also known as *A. billottii*). A dwarf fern that is ideal for rock gardens in coastal districts. It grows naturally in crevices on cliff faces by the Atlantic Ocean. It is similar in appearance and often confused with *Asplenium adiantum-nigrum* but the fronds of the lanceolate spleenwort are narrower towards the base than those of the black spleenwort.

A. marinum (sea spleenwort). A British variety of spleenwort which is tolerant of sea spray. It has glossy green fronds and purplish-brown stems making it a handsome potted plant. If grown indoors it needs humidity. An Australian spleenwort tolerant of seaside conditions is *A. obtusatum*.

A. majus. See *A. flaccidum.*
A. mayi. See *A. flaccidum.*
A. nidus (bird's nest, crow's nest fern). The bird's nest fern is one of the most widely grown epiphytes. Many people are surprised to find that it is a tree dweller like the Platyceriums, because it is seen so often as a low garden feature, or gracing a big pot in a fernery. It is one of the rare ferns whose leaves are entire — most ferns' leaves are cut or dissected into leaflets. It makes an ideal potted plant because the root system is small in relation to the rest of the plant. But to grow it in a pot, plenty of efficient drainage and a light, gritty, porous potting mixture should be provided. In the ground there should be plenty of humus in the soil so that it is easy for its rather delicate root system to penetrate. It is best grown in light shade and broken sunlight.

The fern can be propagated from spores, or if it has outgrown its pot or situation (it does grow very large fronds up to 2 m [6 ft] long and 20 cm [8 in] wide) it can be divided. This is best done in the spring. The plant is cut into four equal portions and the foliage of each should be cut back to about 15 cm (6 in) from the crown before each segment is replanted. Eventually, with reasonable care, each new plant will become symmetrical, but this may take a year or two.

The bird's nest fern is one of the most spectacular ferns. High up in the tree tops of the rainforests of its native south-east Australia it makes a beautiful sight with the sunlight shining through wide, bright green fronds and now and then broken into slivers by the precise lines of the linear sori. This is how it should look, so protect it from strong sunlight and harsh winds that scorch and batter each new batch of fronds and leave the plant looking pathetic, thus giving the species a bad name.

A. polypodium. See *A. falcatum*.

A. ruta-muraria (wall rue spleenwort). A small plant that is common throughout Britain where it is found on rocks and old mortared walls. It can be grown in pots if the drainage is good and is considered hardy in most conditions though it is slow to establish itself.

A. scolopendrium (hart's-tongue fern — also known as *Scolopendrium vulgare, Phyllitis scolopendrium*). This fern has many cultivars including 'Crispum' (deeply frilled like a ruff), 'Cristatum' (fronds terminate in crests or tassels), 'Fimbriata' (deeply and finely fringed, frilled margins), 'Marginatum' (narrow fronds, closely lobed), 'Muricatum' (frilled fronds covered with rough projections all over the surfaces), 'Ramo-cristatum' (narrow, many-times branched fronds terminating in flat crests), 'Undulatum' (frond margins gently undulate) and 'Variegatum'. All are hardy and commonly cultivated plants. They are well known to most gardeners by their strap-like, leathery fronds. These are usually glossy, some with wavy, some with deeply ruffled edges, all with precisely linear sori. The plant is extremely tolerant of most conditions, even frost, but susceptible to overwatering. It can be propagated by inserting basal pieces of the stipe in a propagating mixture.

Asplenium ruta-muraria

Asplenium scolopendrium

Top left: *Humata tyermanni*
Top right: *Lastreopsis hispida*
Bottom: *Microsorium scandens*

Top: *Nephrolepis exaltata* cv. Childsii
Bottom left: *Nephrolepis cordifolia* var. *plumosa*
Bottom right: Close up of *Nephrolepis exaltata* cv. Childsii

Top left and right: *Osmunda regalis*
Bottom left: *Paraceterach muelleri*
Bottom right: *Phlebodium aureum*

Top left: *Pellaea falcata*. Top right: *Pellaea rotundifolia*
Bottom left: *Pityrogramma austroamericana*. Bottom right: *Phymatodes scolopendrium*

A. trichomanes (common spleenwort, maiden-hair spleenwort). Common throughout Britain, this is a low growing, spreading plant with long slender fronds and pinnules of maidenhair fern form which are regularly spaced along the frond. It is hardy and grows well in a rock garden where it will tolerate some sunlight and dry periods. It likes limestone added to its soil in the garden or in a pot.

Asplenium trichomanes

A. viviparum. See *A. daucifolium*.

ATHYRIUM
(lady ferns)

A genus of medium to large growing ferns which are widely distributed throughout the world. It has many forms most of them with delicate and finely divided fronds which give them a soft, attractive appearance. There are many forms suitable for cultivation. The common name is misleading—it comes from the fern's soft appearance, not its sex.

Athyrium australe (austral lady fern). A well established plant of this species will, under ideal conditions, develop a hardy and woody trunk and elongated fronds so that it looks like a tree fern. A species native to subtropic and temperate regions of eastern Australia and New Zealand, it is easily grown given plenty of moisture and protection from the wind.

A. filix-femina. Together with its varieties and cultivars this is probably the most common of all ferns found in the temperate regions of the Northern Hemisphere. The many and beautiful varieties are widely and easily cultivated and grow rapidly. They have been paid many a literary tribute among them Sir Walter Scott's:

> Where the copse wood is the
> greenest,
> Where the fountain glistens sheenest,
> Where the morning dew lies longest,
> There the Lady Fern grows strongest.

Athyrium filix-femina

A. filix-femina **cv. Corymbiferum.** A heavily crested cultivar, the crests dividing in several places to give a bundled tasselled effect. It is small, hardy and easily grown and one of the most sought after species by keen growers.

Athyrium filix-femina cv. Corymbiferum

A. filix-femina **var.** *frizelliae* (the tatting fern). A hardy variety, deciduous in cool-temperature areas. The fronds look like strings of green beads as the pinnae are tiny and bead-like.

Athyrium filix-femina var. *frizelliae*

A. filix-femina **cv. Victoriae.** Found growing wild in Britain in Victorian times and named for the Queen. This is a beautiful and unusually formed fern with very narrow and dainty fronds which can be 1 m (3 ft) or more long; the pinnules form a criss-crossed pattern. Sporelings come true to parent plant form, but have evidently never equalled the parent plant in strength and vigour. It is considered hardy.

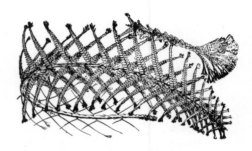

Frond of *Athyrium filix-femina* cv. Victoriae

BLECHNUM
(water ferns in Australia, hard ferns in Britain, rib ferns in the United States)

This large genus of over 200 species is widespread throughout the world. Many of the species have pink new growth and form a distinct caudex with age.

Blechnum brasiliense. The largest species of the *Blechnum* genus grows to about 1 m (3 ft) in height and has a tree fern-like character; the fronds can grow to a diameter of 1.5 m (5 ft). It is easy and not too demanding to grow, but must be kept well watered and the water kept off the fronds. It is a vigorous species, responding particularly to warmth and plenty of light, and will soon outgrow its pot as a house plant. Its natural habitat is the jungles of Brazil and Peru.

B. brasiliense **cv. Crispum.** A medium to large growing fern which is considered tender and needs plenty of protection. The coarse green fronds are wavy and tinged with red when young.

Blechnum brasiliense

B. capense (palm-leaf fern). From the sub-alpine forests of New Zealand, this species has two distinct forms of fronds—the barren ones are glossy with finely serrated edges and the fertile fronds are tall and narrow and covered with sori. It is very variable, the length of the fronds seeming to depend on environmental conditions. Hardy, but grows best in humus rich ground. It does not grow well in a pot.

B. cartilagineum (bristle fern). A terrestrial plant found in eastern Australia and the Philippines. It has large, light green fronds with wavy edges; new growth is often pink. It is an easily grown plant which is hardy in a dry situation. Australian Aborigines used to eat the rhizome.

B. discolor. Also from the sub-alpine forests of New Zealand, this **Blechnum** is semi-hardy. It has narrow fronds varying in length from 30 to 100 cm (1 to 4 ft), glossy green on top and greyish-green or cinnamon underneath. Young fronds are copper coloured. For successful cultivation it needs medium light and to be kept moist.

B. gibbum. A medium sized fern. The deeply cut fronds form a closely knit spiral on top of the erect stem which coarsens and develops into a trunk with age. It is semi-tender requiring medium light and a constantly moist soil and makes a good looking potted plant.

B. nudum (fishbone water fern). A common sight in the mountain areas of Victoria where it forms dense colonies along creek banks. The light green fronds are arranged from a central base in a symmetrical pattern. It is easily grown but requires plenty of moisture.

B. occidentale (hammock fern). Native to the West Indies, Mexico, Central and South America, this small semi-tender member of the **Blechnum** genus has attractive reddish new growth. In cultivation it needs plenty of light and to be kept moist, though this species is more tolerant than others of the genus to drier, more exposed situations.

Blechnum occidentale

B. patersonii (strap water fern). Found in eastern Australia, New Zealand and Fiji this is a small species with strap-like fronds of variable shape. It grows easily in wet, shaded positions.

B. penna-marina (alpine water fern). A hardy, dwarf, creeping species from eastern Australia, New Zealand, South America and sub-Antarctic islands. The fertile fronds are erect and the barren fronds spreading. It is very suited to growing in a pot.

B. spicant (deer fern in the United States, hard fern, ladder fern). A dimorphic fern found widely throughout the Northern Hemisphere.

The barren fronds are glossy green with the pinnae set regularly like the teeth of a comb; the fertile fronds are longer, but again the pinnae, though slimmer, are set in a regular pattern. It is a low growing and hardy species that is tolerant of shade and easy to grow in temperate areas.

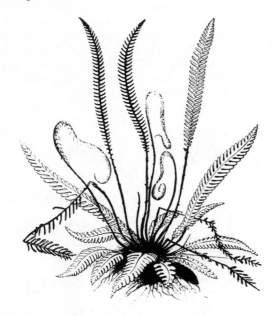

Blechnum spicant

B. watsii (hard water fern). Native to the east coast of Australia, this fern can be found as the main ground cover in the moist mountainous areas of Victoria where, if it runs out of ground space, it will climb the trunk of a tree fern. The new growth is pink. This species is easily grown with a little protection.

BOTRYCHIUM
(moonwort, grape fern)

A genus of about 25 species widely distributed throughout the world though only a few species are cultivated. All moonworts have two fronds only—one barren and one fertile. The spores are carried in clusters like grapes above the single yellow-green, triangular fertile frond. The plant is also unique in that it does not have the usual crozier development of the frond—it develops under the ground and is drawn out by the elongating stem.

Botrychium lunaria (moonwort). This plant is included here because of its value as a fern curiosity and its association with the folklore that has grown around ferns, rather than for its value as a garden or potted plant. It is easy to cultivate once established, but needs some protection if grown in the open ground.

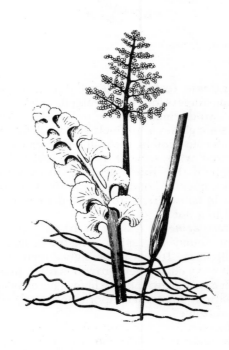

Botrychium lunaria

B. virginianum (rattlesnake fern). A small, hardy, succulent species, the largest of the genus and one of the few Botrychiums cultivated. It is difficult to establish and is best transplanted with a large sod of the original earth intact to protect the fleshy roots. Thereafter it needs plenty of deep soil which is rich in leaf mould, medium light and plenty of moisture.

CAMPTOSORUS

A genus of two species of small, terrestrial ferns that inhabit limestone rocks in North America and north-east Asia.
Camptosorus rhizophyllus (walking fern). A native to North America and north-east Asia, this is a small, hardy, terrestrial fern that is happy with its roots among limestone rocks. The long tapered fronds form new plants when their tips rest on the soil and it will quickly colonise a sheltered rock garden. It makes an easy care and attractive potted plant.

Camptosorus rhizophyllus

CETERACH

A small genus of three species of dwarf, xerophytic ferns found along the Mediterranean coast, central Europe, Britain, North Africa, west Asia and the Himalayas.
Ceterach officinarum (rustyback fern, scaly spleenwort in Britain—also known as *Asplenium ceterach*). A very dwarf, xerophytic species native to Britain, Europe, west Asia and North Africa. It is very hardy and easy to grow, and is especially suited to wall and rock garden growing. The fronds have a leathery texture and are a light sage green. Silver scales which turn brown as they mature

thickly clothe the undersides of the leaf. This fern can recover from dehydration even if the plant appears to have died.

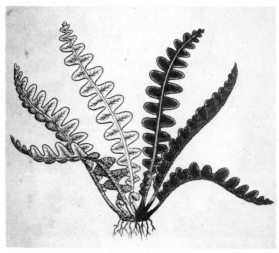

Ceterach officinarum

CRYPTOGRAMMA
(rock brakes)

A genus of four species of small, coarse ferns which grow in rocky alpine and boreal areas (areas where the north winds blow) of Europe, Asia and America.
Cryptogramma crispa (parsley fern). A small, hardy, dimorphic fern which strongly resembles parsley in colour and form. It is considered difficult to cultivate unless the ground is kept continually moist and the fronds are in light shade. It will not tolerate lime but is most at home in rock gardens like its natural habitat, the alpine areas of the Northern Hemisphere.

CULCITA

A genus of about nine species from tropic and subtropic areas of the Southern Hemisphere.

Cryptogramma crispa

Culcita dubia (common ground fern, rainbow fern, false bracken). One of the most common ferns growing wild in eastern Australia where its large, yellow-green fronds clothe the sides of roads and streams. While easily cultivated in open garden situations, it will need room to spread.

CYSTOPTERIS
(bladder ferns)

The ferns of this genus are mostly small and delicate. Only a few are in general cultivation where they are suited to a shaded rock garden. The common name comes from the inflated, hood-like indusium.

Cystopteris fragilis (brittle bladder fern, fragile bladder fern). A fern widely distributed throughout the world. Small and hardy it likes low light and shade. It is suitable as a terrarium plant.

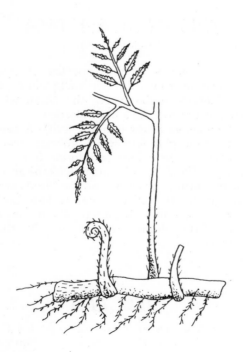

Culcita dubia

Cystopteris fragilis

C. bulbifera (berry bladder fern, bulblet bladder fern). A medium growing species, though the length of the fronds may vary. Bulblets form at the junction of pinna to rachis and develop into new plants. A native of North America, it is a hardy plant and likes a moist to wet situation.

CYRTOMIUM
(holly ferns)

Medium growing ferns with tough, leathery foliage from the tropics and sub-tropics.

Cyrtomium falcatum (house holly fern in the United States, Japanese holly fern in Britain). This species is used extensively as an indoor plant because of its medium size, attractive shiny green leaves, hardiness and tolerance of direct morning and late afternoon sunlight. Both this and its cultivar 'Rochfordianum' need medium to high light and moist conditions and should be kept on the dry side of moist over winter. Both plants are tolerant of drier, exposed positions if they are watered regularly until established.

Cyrtomium falcatum

C. falcatum cv. **Butterfieldii** (Butterfield fern or Japanese holly fern). Similar to the following cultivar but with a slightly smaller leaf form. It is tolerant of low light and humidity.

C. falcatum cv. **Rochfordianum** (Rochford fern). This cultivar has a more pronounced holly shaped leaf and is easy to grow both indoors and out, requiring the same light and moisture conditions as its parent species (above).

DAVALLIA
(hare's foot fern in Australia, rabbit's foot or squirrel's foot in the United States and Britain)

A genus familiar to most gardeners. The species are small to medium growing epiphytes with long, creeping rhizomes covered in soft scales, and grow naturally in tropical areas of Asia and Australia. The fronds of each species are on the whole similar—broad and deeply dissected, some coarse and some very finely divided, tri-angular in shape and supported on wiry stems. Growing in the wild in association with staghorn and elkhorn ferns their rhizomes sometimes penetrate and kill these plants.

Many of the species are deciduous, the fronds turning a lovely golden yellow before dropping. In an ideal growing atmosphere the old fronds may tend to linger so that their deciduous nature is hardly noticeable. If the new fronds appear before the old have dropped off it is a good idea to remove the old to make way for new growth. These plants will also drop their leaves in times of low humidity or drought, which generally makes them a hardy species to cultivate.

Being epiphytes Davallias make ideal ferns for hanging baskets. When well established, several plants will cover the outside of a basket entirely, turning it into an attractive ball of waving fronds for most of the year—without the fronds, a well-established basket is an equally attractive furry mass of criss-crossed rhizomes. Planted in the ground among rocks these ferns form an effective ground cover.

If the creeping rhizomes get themselves in too much of a tangle it is best to break up the clumps, discarding the old, dead parts of the rhizomes, and replant the parts with growing tips. The rhizomes should be planted so that they are resting *on* the soil surface. Put several of the new plants in and around the sides of a basket lined with moss, paper bark, or carpet underfelt, or a basket made of tree fern wood; the roots can quickly establish in these soft media and take moisture and nourishment from all the way around the basket. The new growing tips on the rhizomes can be tied down with raffia or bent wire pegs until they head in the direction you want them to take.

The Davallias make ideal potted and basket plants for the house as they are able to tolerate slightly drier air than most ferns — the firm texture of the rhizome is the reason for this tolerance. Similarly their soil should be kept on the dry side of moist. Propagation is by division of the rhizomes, or by spores sown in the spring.

Davallia denticulata (toothed Davallia). A hardy, but frost tender species which comes from Australia and Asia. Grows happily in the wild in sometimes very exposed positions. It has deeply divided fronds and a thick rhizome covered in light brown scales.

D. fejeensis. A small to medium growing species which is tender, coming as it does from the warm island of Fiji. It is tolerant of most light conditions but needs to be kept on the dry side of moist. Layers of delicate lacy fronds make this an attractive basket or potted plant.

D. fejeensis cv. **Major.** Similar to *D. fejeensis*, but larger. This is a popular but tender species tolerant of most light conditions. It should be kept on the dry side of moist.

D. fejeensis cv. **Plumosa.** (plume Davallia). The most delicate and finely cut of the Davallias. Small to medium growing, it is tolerant of most light conditions, but should be kept on the dry side of moist.

D. mariesii (ball fern). A hardy species from Japan with shiny green fronds. The creeping rhizome is covered with grey-brown, silky scales with white silky tips.

D. pyxidata. A native Australian species, small growing and hardy.

D. trichomanoides (squirrel's foot fern). Native to South-East Asia, Ceylon, Malaysia and Indonesia, this is an easily grown, medium sized species with graceful arching fronds and nut brown scales on the rhizome. A little frost tender, but tolerant of morning and late afternoon sunlight. This is a suitable species for a rock garden as it likes to be kept on the dry side of moist. Its graceful arching fronds also look attractive filling a hanging basket.

Davallia fejeensis

Davallia trichomanoides

DENNSTAEDTIA
(cup ferns)

A genus found throughout the world and considered somewhat primitive. The species all have triangular, finely dissected fronds.

Dennstaedtia davallioides (lacy ground fern). A primitive species endemic to Australia and commonly cultivated as a hardy, attractive pot or garden plant. In its ideal cool protected situation it can become a nuisance in the garden.

Dennstaedtia davallioides

D. puntilobula (hay-scented fern). An adaptable species from North America with long, delicate, tapering fronds and new growth covered in white hairs. The pleasant smell of new mown hay comes from minute glands on the undersides of mature fronds. It is so adaptable that it is considered a weed in some temperature areas.

DOODIA
(rasp ferns, hacksaw ferns)

A worldwide genus of small to medium growing terrestrial ferns. They are hardy and thrive in cultivation, but are slow growing. The fronds are long and tapering at both ends, often harsh to look at and to the touch. New growth is reddish.

Doodia aspera (prickly rasp fern). From Australia where it is common in the eastern states, this fern is hardy and easy to cultivate. New fronds are an attractive bright pink. The mature fronds are rough and harsh and up to 60 cm (2 ft) in length.

Doodia aspera multifida

D. caudata (small rasp fern). From Australia and New Zealand, this is a slender delicate species with dimorphic sterile and fertile fronds. Some fronds extend into a long tail up to 30 cm (1 ft) in length. These fronds tend to weep gracefully thus making this species an ideal one for a basket. Maoris used this fern as a source of perfume. Easily grown, but slow, it needs some shelter in the open ground.

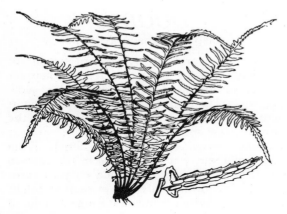

Doodia caudata

DORYOPTERIS

Small ferns mainly from tropical America with maple leaf-like fronds borne on the end of long, shiny stipes.

Doryopteris pedata var. *palmata* (hand fern). A small, slightly tender species which is commonly cultivated. It needs warmth and protection, medium light conditions and some humidity.

D. media (common rasp fern in Australia, hacksaw fern in the United States). A small to medium growing species commonly cultivated. It is slightly tender, requires plenty of light and to be kept on the dry side of moist. New fronds are an attractive purplish-red. This is an easily grown, but slow species.

Doryopteris pedata

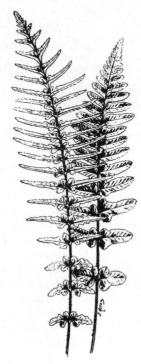

Doodia media

DRYNARIA
(oak leaf ferns)

A genus of about 20 species of medium to large growing ferns from tropical parts of Asia. The species are generally tender. Individual plants form two kinds of leaves — humus collecting oak-like leaves and long, divided foliage leaves.

Drynaria quercifolia (also known as *Polypodium quercifolia*, *Phymatodes quercifolia* and *Polypodium sylvaticum*). A tender species from Malaya, south China, India, Fiji and

north Queensland. It is a lovely species with distinctly dimorphic fronds. In parts of Asia the fern has been used as an astringent and to treat typhoid fever and colds. It needs winter protection in temperate areas, high humidity and well-drained soil. The rhizome should not be planted too deeply and should be anchored firmly to establish a new plant. This species grows best in a big basket or big pot in cultivation.
D. vulgaris. See *Phymatodes scolopendrium*.

DRYOPTERIS
(shield ferns, buckler ferns)

A worldwide genus (though it is now thought that there are no species in Australia) of generally hardy ferns for cultivation. Mostly medium sized plants with thick erect rhizomes and fronds forming a crown.

Dryopteris austriaca spinulosa (broad shield fern, broad buckler fern, toothed wood fern (also known as *D. dilatata, D. spinulosa* var. *dilatata*). A robust, hardy woodland fern with finely cut fronds which are used commercially by florists.

D. dilatata. See *D. austriaca spinulosa*.

D. erythrosora (autumn fern, Japanese shield fern). A hardy and attractive species with glossy, coppery pink new growth. A native of Japan, China and the Philippines, this species will grow in shade or in areas of morning and late afternoon sun.

D. filix-mas (male fern). A hardy species of the Northern Hemisphere which has feathered and crested foliage. It is found growing wild throughout Britain but is rather rare in North America. The plant is very variable and has given rise to many varieties which are universally cultivated. The common name "male fern" comes from its robust appearance as the name "lady fern" (*Athyrium filix-femina*) comes from that fern's delicate air—both common names date from Chaucer's time.

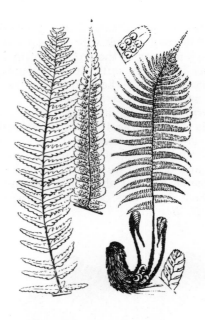

Dryoteris filix-mas

D. marginalis (marginal shield fern, marginal buckler fern). A hardy shade tolerant species native to North America. It forms a short root stock and a single crop of long, dark blueish-green fronds.
D. phegopteris. See *Thelypteris phegopteris*.
D. spinulosa var. *dilatata*. See *D. austriaca spinulosa*.
D. thelypteris. See *Thelypteris palustris*.

GLEICHENIA
(coral ferns, umbrella ferns)

A small genus of about 10 species which grow in many and varied habitats usually with their roots in boggy or damp soil and their scrambling fronds in full sunlight. The genus is instantly recognisable by the unusual fronds which branch and rebranch sometimes over areas of hundreds of metres, forming an impenetrable, tangled mass. On the whole the family is hardy, but difficult to transplant and slow to re-establish.
Gleichenia dicarpa (pouched coral fern, tangle fern). A common, widespread species found

in Australia, New Zealand and South-East Asia. It is easy to cultivate if the roots are kept very moist and the fronds are in some sunlight. It is very difficult to transplant a large species so it is best to concentrate on getting small plants established.

G. microphylla (scrambling coral fern, umbrella fern, parasol fern). A spreading, strong growing species that forms large masses often weighing down low growing shrubs and ferns in its natural habitat along creek banks in Australia, New Zealand and South-East Asia. It is cultivated in the same way as *G. dicarpa*.

Gleichenia dicarpa

GRAMMITIS

A genus of about 150 small epiphytes and lithophytes which grow in tropical and subtropical parts of the world.

Grammitis australis. See *G. billardieri.*

Grammitis billardieri (finger fern —also known as *Grammitis australis*). A species native to Australia, New Zealand, South Africa and South America. The long oblong fronds which can grow up to 16 cm (7 in) give this rock dwelling plant its common name. It is difficult to cultivate.

Grammitis billardieri

GYMNOCARPIUM
(oak ferns)

Small to medium growing ferns from the temperate areas of the world. The fronds are spaced well apart along the long creeping rhizome on very slender stipes.

Gymnocarpium dryopteris (common oak fern

Gymnocarpium dryopteris

—also known as *Polypodium dryopteris*). A worldwide species that has been reclassified many times over the past few decades. The plant is very small with bright, golden green, slender stipes and delicate, three times branched, golden green fronds. It is commonly seen as a ground cover in eastern North America. The new, unfurling fronds are intriguingly like a pawn broker's sign. An ideal and hardy garden plant, it needs plenty of room to spread. It is also suitable for rock garden planting.

HELMINTHOSTACHYS

A genus of one species that grows throughout South-East Asia.
Helminthostachys zeylanica (flowering fern). The palmate sterile fronds borne on a long stipe and the fleshy, fertile frond borne on an offshoot above the sterile fronds give the species the appearance of a flowering plant — hence the common name. The creeping rhizome is eaten as a vegetable in Malaya. This species is easily grown if protected from frost.

Helminthostachys zeylanica

HISTIOPTERIS

A small genus of unusually large robust plants.
Histiopteris incisa (bat's wing fern, oak fern). A large terrestrial creeping fern with big, pale green fronds, the tips of which grow continuously. It likes a cool, moist situation in the ground or in a pot. It is widespread throughout Australia where it can become a pest.

Histiopteris incisa

HUMATA

A genus of about 40 species spread throughout South-East Asia, Polynesia, Malaysia and the Malagasy Republic. All are small to medium growing epiphytic ferns. This genus is closely related to the Davallias, but generally the ferns are smaller.
H. tyermannii (bear's foot fern). A slow growing, semi-tender species from central China needing fairly plentiful light. Grows well and looks good in a basket where it should be kept on the dry side of moist. This is also a suitable species for a rock garden.

Humata tyermannii

HYPOLEPIS

Medium to large sized, rapidly growing, creeping ground ferns with, on the whole finely divided, triangular fronds. Widely distributed throughout the world the genus consists of about 45 species.

Hypolepis millefolium. A species from New Zealand which has probably the most finely cut fronds of any fern. It is easy to grow, but prefers lime-free conditions and protection from extremes of cold.

H. tenuifolia. A large, semi-hardy species from Australia and New Zealand which is easy to grow. It has pale stems covered with soft, white hairs.

LASTREOPSIS

A widely distributed genus of handsome ferns with broad, lacy fronds. Mostly medium sized, terrestrial plants.

Lastreopsis hispida (bristly shield fern). Native to New Zealand, it is a little tender and should be protected from frost and kept

Lastreopsis hispida

Hypolepis tenuifolia

thoroughly moist, but perfectly drained. A beautiful fern that is worth the extra trouble to grow.

L. microsora (creeping shield fern). A vigorous Australian species, dainty looking and semi-tender but easy to grow. It is tolerant of morning and late afternoon sunlight.

LEPTOPTERIS
(crepe ferns)

A small genus of about 60 species from mostly tropical parts of the world. They have filmy fronds borne in a whorl on the crown rather like a tree fern, and a woody trunk up to 1 m (3 ft) high. They are delicate ferns that require the same conditions as filmy ferns, that is shade, plenty of moisture and high humidity. The species *superba* and *hymenophylloides* are listed in old fern books as members of the *Todea* and *Osmunda* genera, to which they are closely related.

Leptopteris hymenophylloides. A species native to New Zealand that is difficult but very rewarding to grow. It requires shade, very high humidity, shelter and moist conditions. A cool or unheated greenhouse can be satisfactory as long as the humidity is kept high—under such conditions the fronds may reach 60 cm (2 ft) in length and 45 cm (18 in) in width, and old specimens may develop a short trunk.

L. superba (Prince of Wales feather). This New Zealand species is considered one of the most beautiful ferns in cultivation, but like the above species it is very demanding to grow and requires the same conditions. The prothallus is hardy and long lived, but the sporophyte is slow to establish. Fine specimens of this species and *L. wilkesiana* can be seen in Kew Gardens, London.

LYGODIUM

A widespread genus of about 40 species whose structure is very complex and differs greatly from that of other ferns. They are, on the whole, vigorous climbing plants that dwell in the rainforest regions of the world.

Lygodium japonicum (Japanese climbing fern). This species with yellow-green leaves is widespread throughout Asia and Australasia. In a sheltered, frost-free position it will twine vigorously and daintily up a support or trail from a basket, looking more like a vine than a fern. It is easy to grow, but good drainage is essential and there should be ample humidity in the atmosphere for the fern to look its best. It is tolerant of morning and late afternoon sunlight.

Leptopteris superba

Lygodium palmatum

L. palmatum (Hartford fern). A dimorphic, climbing fern native to North America where it grows in woodland areas. Though tolerant of low light conditions, it is semi-tender so if grown outside should be protected from frost. The soil should be deep and rich. Give this fern plenty of support on which to climb or a basket from which to cascade.

MARATTIA

A genus of about 60 species of primitive ferns from the tropical areas of Australia, South-East Asia, Polynesia and South Africa. The species are thick and coarse and closely resemble the *Angiopteris* species. They are readily cultivated.

Marattia fraxinea. See *M. salicina.*

M. salicina (potato fern — also known as *M. fraxinea*). A strong growing, large, creeping fern from tropical areas of Queensland and South-East Asia. The fronds have fleshy stipes and may grow up to 4 m (14 ft) long in a protected situation. The plant is hardy to frost when mature. The starchy rhizomes are eaten by Maoris in New Zealand. The tissues turn purple when cut or torn.

MATTEUCCIA

Dimorphic, medium sized ferns from the northern temperate areas of the world.

Matteuccia struthiopteris (ostrich fern). A large, strong and fast growing, easily cultivated fern which is native to Europe and North Africa. The common name comes from the smaller fertile frond-carrying pinnae that form in clusters of tufts, making the plant look like a bundle of ostrich feathers. The species will grow in wet or boggy soils. The fiddleheads are edible (see recipe page 24).

MICROSORIUM

A large genus of typical epiphytes growing on tree trunks and rocks in the wild. They are closely related to the Polypodiums and often referred to as such.

Microsorium diversifolium (kangaroo fern). An easily grown, creeping species from Australia and New Zealand with semi-weeping, extremely variable fronds. It is attractive in a pot if given good drainage and a piece of wood

Marattia salicina

Top: *Platycerium hillii*
Bottom left: *Pteris tremula*
Bottom right: Close up of *Pteris cretica* cv. Childsii

Top left: *Pteris vittata*
Top right: *Pteris quadriaurita* var. *tricolor*
Bottom: *Pteris cretica* cv. Childsii

Top left: *Rumohra adiantiformis*
Top right: *Polystichum setiferum*
Bottom: *Polystichum vestitum*

Top left: *Woodwardia radicans*
Top right: *Pteridium aquilinum*
Bottom: *Thelypteris palustris*

to cling to, and makes a good basket plant. *M. scandens* (fragrant fern—also known as *Polypodium scandens*). A subtropical fern, native to the south-east of Australia and most of New Zealand, which has been reclassified

Microsorium scandens

many times. The semi-weeping fronds are extremely variable. It is a scrambling fern which in the wild almost smothers the upper parts of tree fern trunks and low tree branches. The common name comes from the distinctive but faint aroma of the fresh fronds—it is more pronounced if the frond is dried and crushed. It is easy to grow, tolerant of low light conditions and easy to propagate from spore or division of the rhizome.

NEPHROLEPIS
(fishbone ferns)

A widespread genus of epiphytic ferns which are, on the whole, vigorous,

extraordinarily tolerant of dry air and high temperatures, and easy to grow. If these ferns are grown in a pot it is essential that the soil is well aerated and watering is carried out carefully. It is important that the foliage should not stay wet because it will mat down and the fronds will be lost or disfigured. The soil must be kept on the dry side of moist during the colder months when the plant is not growing actively. The fronds look more lush if the plant is kept slightly rootbound, fertilised regularly and if there is ample humidity in the atmosphere. An occasional yellowing of the old fronds is quite natural in a plant that is growing vigorously—they need only to be trimmed off regularly to allow light and air to reach the new growth. Also remove any plantlets that revert to plain fishbone-type foliage as they are strong growing and can take over.

Members of the *Nephrolepis* species have long, slender scaly stems or stolons which produce new plants when they touch the soil, so to propagate new plants give the parent plenty of room to spread and take root and the resultant baby plants can be then lifted when they have made two or more fronds. They should be placed in small pots that will just contain the rootball. The species can also be propagated easily by division, meristem culture and spores (except the true Boston fern, *N. exaltata* var. *bostoniensis*, and its derivatives, which do not produce spores).

Most *Nephrolepis* species and cultivars are considered hardy for the amateur grower to cultivate inside the house, in the unheated greenhouse or outside in sheltered areas.

Nephrolepis cordifolia (tuber sword fern, common fishbone fern in southern parts of Australia, herringbone fern). This species is widely distributed throughout the world from the tropics to the subtropics. It has colonised freely in many areas. The fronds are up to 1 m (3 ft) long, narrow and a dull green. The pinnae are narrow and well spaced at the top and bottom of each frond but tend to overlap in the centre. This species is distinguished from the *N. exaltata* species in that it produces oval, brown scaly tubers on subterranean stolons. It is hardy, fast growing, very easy to cultivate and will tolerate long periods of cold and full sunlight. It can be propagated by means of the tubers which will form new growth if separated from the parent plant. A variety, *N. cordifolia* var. *plumosa*, is also very easy to grow. Its long and attractive fronds are displayed well particularly when grown in a basket.

Nephrolepis cordifolia var. *plumosa*

N. exaltata (sword fern, fishbone fern). Found in temperate and tropical parts of Asia, Africa, Australia and the Americas, this species was introduced to cultivation from Jamaica in 1793 and quickly became a popular greenhouse plant with over 100 cultivars recorded to date. The fronds, which are larger and longer than those of *N. cordifolia*, are generally fairly stiff, dark green and will grow indefinitely. Growth is softer and more arching if the plant is cultivated in the shade and growth is generally better with extra heat and humidity.

N. exaltata var. *bostoniensis* (Boston fern). This fern, a descendant of the sword or fishbone fern, *N. exaltata*, has a fascinating history. In 1895 a florist near Boston found among his sword ferns a new variety with softer, more graceful and longer foliage, and many more leaves. It was greatly admired and was soon being sold in thousands. The mutation, which was evidently not due to hybridisation but to a change of genes, went wild and almost simultaneously there appeared among the many thousands of Boston ferns in widely separate localities a half dozen strikingly different plants whose leaves were ruffled and frilled in multiple divisions. After this there was a constant succession of new and improved varieties so that altogether more than 200 named varieties have come from this one extraordinary fern. At least 100 of these have been recognised as different.

Nephrolepis exaltata cv. Childsii

Other commonly and easily grown *N. exaltata* cultivars are: cv. Verona, which has yellow-green, lacy fronds; cv. Childsii, with luxurious, massed leaflets; cv. Gretnae, cv. Rooseveltii and cv. Randolpholii, all of which have very long fronds and look beautiful in hanging baskets; cv. Elegantissima and cv. Whitmanii, the very lacy members of the family; cv. Hilsii, which has vigorous, coarse-textured, pendulous fronds each of which has a variation of dark to light green and wavy leaflets; and cv. Smithii and cv. Susi Wong, which are the outstandingly superfine varieties.

ONOCLEA
(sensitive ferns)

Coarse-looking terrestrial ferns from North America. Dimorphic with broad, triangular barren fronds and fertile fronds like clusters of beads.
Onoclea sensibilis (bead fern, American oak fern). One of the most common ferns in North America. Very variable and so adaptable and fast growing that it can become a nuisance in the garden. The individual pinnae sometimes resemble an oak leaf, hence one common name. The species name comes from its sensitivity to early frosts. It is hardy, but needs to be kept on the wet side of moist as it grows naturally in wet or boggy soil.

Onoclea sensibilis

OPHIOGLOSSUM
(adder's tongue ferns)

A worldwide genus included in this list because it is an interesting rather than a cultivated fern and for its historical and mystical associations mentioned in an earlier chapter. There are usually only two fronds, the fertile one growing from the base of the stalk-like barren frond.
Ophioglossum englemanii, O. lusitanicum and *O. vulgatum.* All are difficult to grow and seldom seen out of their natural habitats.

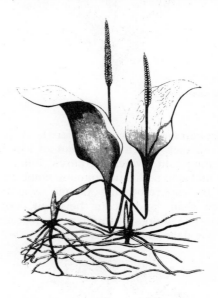

Ophioglossum vulgatum

OSMUNDA
(royal ferns)

Distributed throughout the world, they are medium to large growing ferns some of which form majestic crowns of fronds. In their natural habitat they are found in damp places where there is deep rich soil. The masses of coarse, fibrous roots that these ferns make are collected and used as a growing medium/compost by orchid growers. All species will grow in areas of morning and late afternoon sunlight.

Osmunda cinnamomea. A hardy, shade tolerant, large growing, North American fern that must be kept thoroughly and constantly moist. The species is dimorphic and its name comes from the fertile fronds, which are dark green when young and a bright cinnamon brown when ripe.

Osmunda cinnamomea

O. claytoniana (interrupted fern). A large, hardy species which is tolerant of low light conditions but which requires constantly moist and acid soil. The common name comes from the spore-bearing pinnae which are shorter than, and occur between, normal pinnae. The spores of this fern remain fertile for a few days only.

Osmunda claytoniana

O. regalis (royal fern). One of the largest of the terrestrial ferns of the temperate world, it is hardy and shade tolerant but requires constantly and thoroughly moist and acid soil conditions. It will thrive in boggy conditions. The fronds colour prettily in autumn. A common misnomer is "flowering fern" which comes from the resemblance of the fertile fronds to seedheads of flowering plants. *O. regalis* has escaped in New Zealand and is colonising in swamps around Auckland. It was a very fashionable fern in Victorian times when the English countryside was almost picked clean of it.

Osmunda regalis

PARACETERACH

A genus of a single species which is found only in northern Queensland.
Paraceterach muelleri. A small fern found

growing among rocks in northern Queensland. It is not commonly cultivated but is interesting in its ability to resist drought by curling its fronds and to recover completely after rain. It needs warmth and protection to grow well.

Pellaea falcata

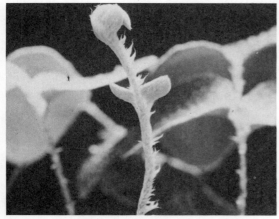

Paraceterach muelleri

P. rotundifolia (New Zealand cliff brake, button fern). A small spreading, xerophytic fern that is fairly hardy. Button shaped pinnae make it very attractive and popular as a cultivated plant. As with others in the genus, this species should be kept on the dry side of moist.

PELLAEA
(brake, cliff brake, rock brake)

Mainly small growing, rock dwelling, xerophytic ferns that are adapted to survive in dry climates. The fronds are usually fishbone-like in formation and the developing croziers like a shepherd's crook. It is a large genus, the plants growing in the dry, subtropical areas of the world,

Pellaea atropurpurea (purple cliff brake). A small, hardy species from North America which grows well in a pot or in a rock garden with some exposure to sunlight. The fronds are blue-green and the stems purple-brown. Plants should be kept on the dry side of moist. This species is tolerant of limestone conditions.

P. falcata (sickle fern, Australian cliff brake). An easily grown, fairly hardy Australian species with elongated, shiny green fronds bearing neatly arranged pinnae. Plants should be kept on the dry side of moist and will tolerate some sun.

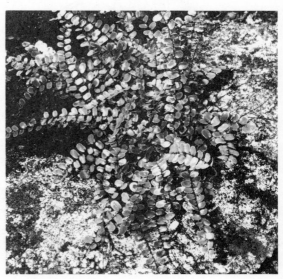

Pellaea rotundifolia

P. viridis var. **viridis** (green cliff brake). A delicate and slightly tender **Pellaea** from subtropical areas of North America with thin lance-like pinnae. One of the largest members of this genus, it needs plenty of light and to be kept on the dry side of moist.

PHLEBODIUM

A small genus of only two species of ferns from tropical America and only recently differentiated from those of the *Polypodium* genus.

Phlebodium aureum (golden polypody—also known as *Polypodium aureum*). A large growing species with deeply cut leaves up to 25 cm (10 in) across and 40 cm (36 in) long. The rhizome is thick and densely covered with orange-brown fur. The fronds are a soft blue-green and are seen to good advantage in a basket or pot. This species is easy to grow, semi-tender, quite tolerant of some sunlight in mornings and late afternoons and dry or exposed situations.

Phlebodium aureum

PHYLLITIS
(hart's-tongue ferns)

Small, evergreen ferns with tongue-shaped fronds found in temperate areas of the Northern Hemisphere. Individual species in cultivation are classified under the genus *Asplenium*.

P. scolopendrium. See *Asplenium scolopendrium.*

PHYMATODES

A small genus of ferns which are very similar in structure to those of the *Microsorium* genus. Several species have been moved from one genus to the other over the past few decades.

Phymatodes quercifolia. See *Drynaria quercifolia.*

Phymatodes scolopendrium (wart fern—also known as *Drynaria vulgaris, Polypodium scolopendrium*). This fern which is found in sub-tropical areas of the world has been classified under several genera and assigned many different species names. The creeping rhizome is a waxy green and irregularly covered with dark brown, stiff, hair-like scales. The deeply lobed fronds are a dark emerald green and the fertile ones "warted" on their upper surface due to the deeply depressed sori on the underside. It is a medium growing, easily cultivated plant whose only special requirements are a loose growing medium rich in humus and with good drainage. It also needs good light and thorough watering.

Phymatodes scolopendrium

PITYROGRAMMA
(goldback, silverback ferns)

Dense yellow and white powder on the back of the fronds make this xerophytic genus very attractive. The species on the whole are small to medium growing, tender because they come from the African and American tropics but tolerant of morning and late afternoon sunlight. The genus is now widespread throughout the world as many species have naturalised.

Pityrogramma austroamericana (gold fern —also known as *P. chrysophylla*). A species originally native to South America and the West Indies, but like the silver fern, it has naturalised in many countries. It is sometimes called the "king of the gold ferns" and is a very attractive plant. A dense rich gold or creamy white, waxy powder forms on the unfurling croziers and the undersides of the fronds. It is a tender, medium growing plant, and only grows readily with plenty of light and moist to dry soil conditions.

Pityrogramma austroamericana

P. calomelanos (silver fern). A species that is native to South America, but has naturalised in many countries of the world so that its origins have almost been lost. The fronds have a fine, lacy look and the undersides are covered with a silver-white powder. The plant is tender, needs plenty of light and moist to dry conditions to grow readily.

P. chrysophylla. See *P. austroamericana.*

P. hybrida. A very successful hybrid of the above two species which has pale yellow-green fronds with gold powdering on the undersides. It is considered more beautiful than both of its parents, luxurious and graceful. It is semi-hardy and the fronds are relatively tolerant of dry air, but the roots must be kept moist and the plant transferred to new containers frequently to accommodate the fast growing root system.

PLATYCERIUM
(staghorn, elkhorn and moosehorn ferns)

A genus of lithophytic or epiphytic ferns which is unique in the fern world for shape, form and habit. There are about 17 species found mainly in the tropics of South America, Africa, Asia and Australia. Several cultivars are in existence. The species vary in size from the small *P. madagascariense* which is about 30 cm (12 in) overall to the giant *P. wilhelimae-reginae* with a shield front over 2 m (7 ft) across and fertile fronds that hang down to almost 2 m (7 ft). The different species are often hard to identify as some plants may take from five to seven years to produce their first fertile fronds, which even then are often variable.

The Platyceriums are dimorphic plants. The flattened sterile fronds are at the back and base of the plant. These fronds go brown and brittle with age so that there is often only a skeleton left, finely veined and net-like. New ones have a dense wax-like look and feel and gradually spread out like a beautiful plate over the base of the plant. The fertile fronds which hang down in front of the plant are erect and multi-branched, resembling the antlers of a deer. They are a delicate green and their tips are covered with a downy pubescence of a paler green. As these fronds mature they become quite bluish in some species and the lower back half becomes covered in the brown velvet of the spore cases.

They grow naturally in the rainforest areas of the world where, high up in the trees, they lead an ethereal existence entangled and entwined with vines and climbers. They grow, too, on old logs, rocks and fallen trees, feeding on the decaying matter of their host, or wrapped around the fibrous trunks of other ferns in a relationship that is of mutual benefit. They are not parasites; there is no such unlovely species in the fern world. Their aerial roots get food from the decaying matter trapped in their own leaf systems or the bark and crevices of their host. Rainwater is stored here too, so that they are resistant to long periods of drought. They are superbly designed for the job of "catching" their food;

the huge nest leaves at the back of the plant are shield-like and tilted outwards at their top, trapping and directing falling debris to the depths of the plant where it breaks down into a rich humus and readily available plant food.

The Platyceriums grow naturally on trees with non-shedding bark like those of the fig, cedar, sassafras and coachwood families, and occasionally on rocks. In cultivation they can be grown on boards fixed to walls or trees, or fixed directly onto a tree that does not shed its bark. To attach a plant to a tree use copper or galvanised wires that will not rust. Do not wrap the wires around the tree's trunk because they may cause damage if they cut into the life-giving cambium layer just beneath the bark. Fix the wire to nails driven straight into the tree's wood. Magnificent old staghorn and elkhorn ferns, fixed in this way originally, are often seen wrapped right around the trunk of a supporting tree so that all signs of their support have lost in the depths of their green.

If grown on a board support, it is important that the board be made of stout hardwood and that the plant be fixed firmly to it so that constant movement will not dislodge the developing roots. Do this by nailing the fern to the board with long nails after first driving the nail through an improvised washer made of leather or rubber. Make sure that the base of the plant is very secure because it is from here that the anchoring roots will develop. The top of the plant should project forward slightly to form a V-shape at the back, designed to channel the rotted leaf mould and other decayed matter to the roots. Nature has designed the Platyceriums perfectly for this job so you should understand it to cultivate them successfully. Pack a generous amount of sphagnum moss between the fern and the board to give the roots something in which to shelter until the natural fibrous matter accumulates. The organic matter and water is all that is needed to maintain the plant—no soil is necessary.

If the fern is placed so that it is growing away from trees or in a place where organic matter will not collect naturally, feed it with handfuls of well-rotted leaf mould and old cow manure. Tuck this food down behind the old nest leaves. An old banana skin is a rich source of nitrogen if fed to the plant a few times a year. Do not be tempted to use chemical fertilisers in powdered form as any undissolved granules may collect in the joints of the old fronds, burning them and setting up an ideal situation for rot and fungus attacks.

In the treetops the epiphytes receive plenty of the available rainfall, but this water drains through the aerial roots very quickly. To recreate these conditions in cultivation, the ferns should be watered thoroughly, but not constantly. A state of constant wetness at the base of the plant behind the shield fronds encourages rot. Use the hose to water thoroughly all over, or, if the plant is small enough, take it down and soak it, supporting board and all, until it is saturated. Do not be tempted to sprinkle the plant every time the garden is watered as this will keep it constantly wet, but perhaps sprinkle around it on a hot day to increase the humidity. Several days after a good watering the outer fronds may feel dry to the touch, but check by pressing firmly with the fingers on the base of the lower fronds. If water oozes out, the plant is wet enough and should be left alone for a few more days. Some growers actually wait until the fertile fronds look limp before watering.

It is very important to see that overhead eaves or hanging baskets do not drip constantly onto epiphytic ferns, as this will, again, encourage constant wetness.

These ferns can be propagated by cutting established clumps into sections when a number of plantlets have formed on their bases. Buds or young plantlets bearing several shield fronds can be removed safely from the parent plant and mounted individually on boards or planted out into pots. Use a sharp knife to cut beneath and around the oldest shield frond of the young plant and, if possible, take a small section of the base fronds of the parent plant with the section. All the ferns of the *Platycerium* genus, except *P. veitchii*, are also easily propagated by spores.

Platycerium alcicorne. See *P. bifurcatum*.

P. bifurcatum (common staghorn in the United States, elkhorn in Australia—also known as *P. alcicorne*). A species native to Australia, where it is the most common and most widespread species, Lord Howe Island, New Caledonia and Papua New Guinea. The kidney shaped, deep green shield fronds grow tightly pressed against layers of old fronds which turn brown very quickly. The fertile, pendulous fronds branch into two or three parts and hang down as they mature. The spores form in irregular patches covering all or most of the tips. This species is very hardy, often tolerating temperatures as low as -6°C (25°F). It grows very easily. Old plants often form huge clumps that need strong support, or whole limbs of trees and sometimes trees themselves will fall under the accumulated weight.
P. grande. See *P. superbum.*
P. hillii (northern elkhorn). A native to northeast Australia, this fern is easily confused with *P. bifurcatum*. The top edge of the shield frond is almost uncut or has shallow lobes. The spores form in irregular patches covering the underside of the last section of the lobes on the fertile fronds. This species is hardy and as easily grown as *P. bifurcatum* but is not as frost resistant.

Platycerium hillii

P. superbum (staghorn, in Australia, elkhorn or moosehorn in the United States—also known as *P. grande*). Until recently this was known as *P. grande*, a species found in the Philippines, but it is now known to be a different species. The shield fronds are fan shaped and divided at irregular intervals at the top. The major veins show attractively through the fronds. Fertile fronds are light green, thin, narrow and pendulous. They fork at less than half of their length and the spores are carried in a large patch at the point of the first fork. This fern does not produce plantlets so can only be reproduced by means of its spores.

Platycerium superbum

P. veitchii (silver elkhorn). The popular name comes from the whitish-green colour caused by the tiny matted hairs which cover the spore patches on the deep green fertile fronds. The wide shield fronds are deeply and irregularly lobed and turn brown quickly. The fertile fronds are stiff and grow mostly pointing upwards; the spore patch is on the underside of the last section of the tapering eight-lobed fronds. It is a rare and beautiful plant in its natural habitat, the low rainfall areas of northern Queensland. The thick fleshy texture of the plant and the dense hairs help it to conserve moisture and withstand long periods of dryness. Easily grown and hardy under cultivation, this species is also drought and frost resistant, but requires a higher light situation than the Platyceriums listed above.

Platycerium veitchii

POLYPODIUM
(hare's foot fern)

A very large and diverse group of ferns, most of which are distributed in the tropical and subtropical parts of the world. All of them have a creeping rootstock. Most of the species in cultivation are epiphytes and are best grown in baskets with good drainage, a light, open soil mix and a gentle flow of air around the fronds. Because of the tropical and subtropical origins of most species, they are tender or semi-tender and are therefore better off grown indoors or in the glasshouse in cool temperate areas. They will tolerate minimum night temperatures of 15°C (60°F). They are also tolerant of medium to high light conditions, bright diffused sunlight and dry indoor atmospheres, but grow better with some humidity.

Australian species previously classified as *Polypodium* are now classified under other genera including *Drynaria, Grammitis, Goniophlebium Microsorium, Platycerium* and *Pyrrosia*.

Polypodium angustifolium. An epiphyte whose 30-45 cm (12-18 in) dark green and bronze fronds are narrow and pointed. The creeping rhizome spreads just underneath the soil so that it is not evident. This species looks best and grows best in a basket where it should be protected from dry and cold winds, direct sunlight and freezing weather. It will, however, tolerate extremely strong light but needs humidity.

P. aureum. See *Phlebodium aureum.*

P. australe. See *P. vulgare.*

P. dryopteris. See *Gymnocarpium dryopteris.*

P. goniophlebium cv. **Knightiae** (knight's polypody). A large, deciduous fern which is semi-tender and very different from the species of which it is a cultivar. The species is a magnificent fern whose very long, simply pinnate fronds give it a weeping character. The cultivar has compound feather-like pinnae. It is not difficult to grow and should be planted in a basket to show it off.

P. heracleum. See *Aglaomorpha heraclea.*

P. integrifolium cristatum crested climbing bird's nest fern). A native to Indonesia and tropical Asia where it grows on trees rather like the *Asplenium nidus*. The complex fronds have ripples along the edges and completely irregular projections. These grow to about 1 m (3 ft), becoming pendulous as their length and weight increase. This fern requires warmth and humidity at all times but otherwise is easy to grow in the shade if given regular watering.

P. interjectum. See *P. vulgare.*

P. phegopteris. See *Thelypteris phegopteris.*

P. phyllitidis. Native to tropical America, this species resembles the hart's-tongue fern, *Asplenium scolopendrium*. The smooth fronds grow in clumps from the underground rhizome and may be from 30 to 90 cm (12 to 36 in) in length, almost without a stipe. It is hardy, though it does require some protection from frost and grows well in the ground, in a basket or in a pot. In should be grown in shade with medium light and kept moist.

P. scandens. See *Microsorium scandens.*

P. scolopendrium. See *Phymatodes scolopendrium.*

P. sylvaticum. See *Drynaria quercifolia.*

P. vulgare (wart fern) This species is subject to much conjecture—it is often referred to as *P. interjectum* and *P. australe* and often the three species are considered to be quite distinct. It is a slow growing, creeping fern which inhabits woodlands, stony ground and dry stone walls in Britain, south and south-west Europe and South Africa, and it is widespread in North America. It is easy to cultivate but the soil must be well drained. The common name comes from the appearance of indentations on the upper surface of the frond which are formed by the deeply recessed sori on the underside.

Polypodium vulgare

P. vulgare var. *ramosum* (common polypody). A variety of *P. vulgare* found throughout Britain where it grows in hedgebanks, mossy rocks and sometimes as an epiphyte in trees and rock walls. The fronds of this plant branch repeatedly from the base, but are very variable. It is a small growing plant that is hardy and easy to cultivate, and attractive if grown well. It requires a shady, damp area, but take care that the ground is not continually wet.

POLYSTICHUM
(shield fern)

A large and widespread genus of generally hardy, tough, leathery ferns, given their common name because of the prominent sheild-like indusia. They are small to medium growing ferns that form a cluster of filigreed fronds on top of an erect rhizome. Many cultivars and varieties are in cultivation.

Polystichum acrostichoides (Christmas fern, dagger fern). A hardy, medium sized species with glossy, dagger shaped fronds in shades of blue-green with stipes covered in rusty brown harsh scales. The new fronds are covered in glistening white scales and are used for cut foliage in the United States. This species is slow growing and shade tolerant.

P. aculeatum (hard shield fern). A strong growing hardy species that is fairly common in Britain. The lower part of the stipe is densely clothed in large brown scales. One of its varieties, the hardy *P. aculeatum pulcherrimum gracillimum*, is an extremely beautiful fern; the fronds are incredibly delicate with the hair-like pinnules ending in splayed tassels.

Polystichum aculeatum

Polystichum aculeatum

P. polyblepharum. See **P. setosum.**
P. proliferum (mother shield fern). This is a hardy species endemic to Australia. With age the rhizome forms a thick trunk covered in shiny brown scales which continue up the base of the stipe. It can be propagated from the many plantlets that form at the end of the fronds.
P. setiferum (soft shield fern). The rootstock of this fern is stout and often develops subsidiary crowns from buds on the frond bases. The croziers are covered in glistening white scales which mature to brown. Considered hardy and easy to grow it is tolerant of low light and needs to be kept moist. Many varieties of this species are in cultivation.

Polystichum setiferum

P. setosum (also known as **P. polyblepharum**). A semi-hardy species from Japan which requires plenty of light and moist soil. The fronds are deep green and lacy and the croziers appear to droop, giving them the appearance of a "tassel" and making the whole plant look as if it has dried out and needs watering.
P. tsus-simense (dwarf leather fern, Tsusima holly fern). A small, compact species from Japan and China with sharply cut, triangular fronds. It is hardy and particularly useful in terrariums because of its small size. It also makes a good potted plant and a rock garden plant.
P. vestitum (prickly shield fern). An easily grown shield fern that is native to New Zealand and adaptable to most situations being intolerant only of hot conditions.

Polystichum vestitum

PTERIDIUM
(brackens)

The classification of these ferns is a rather contentious issue among botanists. They are found throughout the world in a wide variety of habitats, but always where the soil is well drained. The brackens are well known for their ability to invade and render useless vast areas of pasture land by means of their slender, wide-creeping, underground rhizomes. They have proved difficult to cultivate and resent transplanting.

Pteridium aquilinum (common bracken in Britain and the Northern Hemisphere—also known as *Pteris aquilinum*). Research into this fern in Europe has revealed cases of poisoning to cattle and horses; although the Australian plant (*P. esculentum*) is different, the poisonous effects appear to be the same. Some species of the *Pteridium* genus are cultivated. These include *P. aquilinum, P. crispum, P. cristatum, P. caudatum, P. latiusculum* (eastern bracken), *P. pubescens* (western bracken).

Pteridium aquilinum

P. esculentum (Austral bracken, common bracken in Australia). This species is widely distributed in particular throughout Australia where it is always considered a nuisance. However, it is difficult to cultivate. The rhizomes are rich in starch and are used as a source of food in some countries; it is a staple of the diet of the natives of the Canary Islands, New Zealand, the Society Islands and Australia.

PTERIS
(brakes)

A large genus of ferns from the tropical and subtropical areas of the world. Most of the 250 or so species and their many named cultivars and varieties are much sought after. "Pteris" comes from the Greek "pteron" meaning feather, an allusion to the shape of the frond. The true species and the true varieties do not produce a great deal of variation in form or shape.

Pteris aquilinum. See *Pteridium aquilinum.*

P. argyraea. See *P. quadriaurita* var. *argyraea.*

P. cretica (Cretan brake, ribbon brake). A fast growing small to medium sized fern. In its native Crete, it is found growing in the wild on moist limestone walls in the shade, where humidity is high and rainfall is ample. It is considered to be semi-hardy, needing protection from extremes of cold, a high light intensity and an open soil mix. Given these conditions it is easy to grow. It will tolerate morning and late afternoon sunlight and survives better in drier, more exposed positions than do most ferns.

P. cretica var. *albo-lineata.* Popular in Victorian times this cultivar of the *P. cretica* has a handsome broad band of creamy white down the centre of each wavy leaflet. Cultivation similar to that of *P. cretica* but should be kept out of direct sunlight.

Pteris cretica

P. cretica cv. **Childsii**. A hybrid, clump-forming fern that is always sterile and so can only be propagated by division. It requires protection from the cold and high light levels. Cultivation similar to that of *P. cretica.*

Pteris cretica cv. Childsii

P. cretica cv. **Parkeri**. A cultivar of *P. cretica* with broad, finely toothed leaflets. Cultivation similar to that of *P. cretica.*

P. cretica cv. **Rivertoniana**. A medium sized variable fern which grows continuously. The light green fronds are feathery like carrot tops. Variation occurs as crests on the pinnae. This species will tolerate strong light, but does best in partial shade. Cultivation similar to that of *P. cretica.*

P. cretica cv. **Wimseti-Multiceps** (skeleton fern). This cultivar is evergreen, creeping and variable. The popular name comes from the skeletal, fragile look of the mature fronds. Cultivation similar to that of *P. cretica.*

P. dentata (toothed brake —also known as *P. flabellata, P. flaccida*). A medium to large growing brake, similar to, but finer than, *P. tremula*. Requires moist conditions and is relatively easy to grow.

P. ensiformis (slender brake in Australia). A compact, hardy species native to Australia where it grows in quite saline conditions on river foreshores. It is easy to grow. This fern has given rise to several cultivars with variegation in the foliage and just as easy to grow as the parent plant.

P. ensiformis cv. **Evergemiensis**. A variegated and much sought after form of *P. ensiformis* (slender brake), a native Australian fern. This cultivar looks almost pure white, but on closer inspection the silver-white markings contrast beautifully with the dark green of the rest of the frond. It is a small growing fern, slightly tender, which requires medium light conditions and to be kept moist.

P. ensiformis var. *victoriae* (Victorian brake, queen's fern). A dimorphic, variegated fern that comes originally from India. It is much sought after as a cultivated plant as it is small growing and ideal for a pot. Cultivation same as above.

P. flabellata. See *P. dentata.*

P. flaccida. See *P. dentata.*

P. longifolia. See *P. vittata.*

P. multifida (Chinese, spider or Huguenot fern—also known as *P. serrulata*). A small, quite hardy fern that has given rise to many crested forms and varieties including *P. multifida* cv. Cristata and *P.m.* var. *angustata* which is particularly valued for its adaptability. Easy to grow in the garden or in a pot. It also makes a good house or rock garden plant. This species, its cultivars and varieties like the addition of calcium to the soil.

Pteris multifida var. *angustata*

P. quadriaurita var. *argyraea* (silver brake, striped brake—also known as *P. argyraea*). A large growing fern with blue-green fronds banded with silver down the centre. The lower leaflets are beautifully shaped. The fern is semi-tender and so requires some protection and should be kept moist. Another variegated form has red colouring in the fronds.

Pteris quadriaurita var. *argyraea*

P. serrulata. See *P. multifida.*
P. tremula. A large, fast growing fern native to Australia, New Zealand, Norfolk Island and Fiji, which is now cultivated throughout the world. It is easy to grow, making a handsome pot plant or a good fill-in in the garden as it propagates so readily from the copious amounts of sori carried on the fronds. It will grow in a moderately sunny position with the soil kept on the dry side of moist. A point to watch—the crown sometimes rises above the soil, exposing the feeding roots and making them susceptible to dehydration. A mulch around the crown, not over it, will protect these roots.
P. tripartita (giant brake in Australia, trisect brake in the United States). A very large, tender species of the *Pteris* genus which is easily grown in warm areas with medium light and moist conditions. Best grown in the ground because of the large fronds—they can be up to 2.5 m (8 ft) long.

P. vittata (Chinese brake, ladder brake, rusty brake—known commercially as *P. longifolia*). A widespread species found throughout tropical and temperate areas of Asia, Africa and Australia. It is a fast growing, easily cultivated, medium sized, dark green, graceful fern that will tolerate high light conditions and resents complete shade. It is hardy in slightly exposed and dry conditions.

Pteris vittata

PYROSSIA
(felt ferns)

A genus of about 100 epiphytic species from tropical rainforest areas of Africa, South America and south-east Australia. All species have simple fleshy fronds and are hardy and drought resistant despite their rainforest origins. They have minute hairs on their fronds which cut down their water loss. The species of this genus make very good rock garden plants.
Pyrossia lingua (tongue fern, Japanese felt fern). A small, slow growing, creeping fern with thick, leathery fronds. It is semi-hardy to semi-tender and easily cultivated. Ideal for a pot and looks particularly good when encouraged to grow around the base of a basket. There are a great many cultivars of this fern, one of which has a yellow variegation.

Pyrossia lingua

P. rupestris (rock felt fern). A hardy, easily grown, dimorphic fern which is found in the rainforests and open forests of south-east Australia. The fronds will shrivel in times of drought but recover with rain. An epiphyte, it will creep over rocks in the ground or be happy in a basket.

RUMOHRA
(leather ferns)

Medium sized terrestrial or epiphytic ferns native to the tropics south of the Equator. Some are lithophytic, growing on rocks and cliff faces.

Rumohra adiantiformis (leather fern in the United States, leathery shield fern or shield hare's foot in Australia). The common name comes from the coarse looking fronds. They are used frequently by florists because they last for weeks when cut and placed in water. Despite its coarse fronds it is a handsome durable plant for the house or for the garden, where because of its creeping habit it will cover a larger space. In conditions of high humidity it will climb trees, as in New Zealand, where it is often confused with some Davallias and Polystichums. It is semi-hardy to semi-tender, requiring medium light conditions and moist to dry soil. Tolerant of morning and late afternoon sunlight, it does well in slightly dry and exposed positions.

Scolopendrium vulgare. See *Asplenium scolopendrium*.

Rumohra adiantiformis

STENOCHLAENA
(climbing fern)

A genus of dimophic, climbing ferns from the rainforests of Malaysia and Africa, with only one species found in Australia.

Stenochlaena palustris

Top: *Cyathea cooperi*
Bottom left: *Cyathea dealbata*
Bottom right: *Cyathea australis*

Top left and right: One of the filmy ferns, *Trichomanes radicans*
Bottom: *Selaginella grandis,* a representative of the fern allies

Stenochlaena palustris (climbing swamp fern). This Australian species is easy to propagate and to grow. It requires shade but plenty of light, and because of its swamp origins should be kept very moist but well drained as it is an epiphyte. If properly managed, its rampant growth, unusual in the fern world, makes it a very rewarding fern. It will fill a basket beautifully and quickly and is an unusual plant with which to cover a shaded pergola. It is tender and needs protection from frost. The old fronds are shiny with finely serrated margins and new fronds are copper coloured, making it a very handsome plant when massed.

STICHERUS

(fan ferns, umbrella ferns)

A genus of bushy ferns with umbrella-like fronds which is not cultivated much outside Australia.

Sticherus flabellatus

Sticherus flabellatus (shiny fan fern, umbrella fern). A very slow growing but robust fern that branches in umbrella-like fashion in one to four tiers. In its natural habitat, in Eastern Australia, New Guinea and New Zealand, it lies in great tangled masses like beautifully soft mists, on top of low growing shrubs. It

makes an attractive plant for a large pot in a moist garden position but it should be grown from small plants as large specimens resent disturbance and will very often not recover.

S. tener (silky fan fern). Very similar to *S. flabellatus* in habit, growth and cultivation. Its fronds are a shiny light green with entire pinnules (*S. flabellatus* has serrated pinnules).

TECTARIA

A genus of about 200 medium to large growing ferns with coarse pale green fronds. The species grow natually in tropical and subtropical parts of the world.

Tectaria gemmifera (button fern in the United States, snail fern in Australia—also known as *T. cicutaria* in the trade). The common name comes from the masses of buds which are produced on the fronds. New plants may be

Tectaria gemmifera

easily propagated from the buds which are in a well-developed stage by the time they are shed from the mother plant (each bud already has several well developed croziers and a scaly exterior to protect it from dryness and infection). It is a medium sized fern that is semi-tender because of its tropical origins. It needs medium light conditions and to be kept moist.

THELYPTERIS
(wood fern, hay fern)

A worldwide genus of about 800 species of usually medium sized ferns with narrow fronds borne in clusters along a creeping rhizome.

Thelypteris hexagonoptera (southern beech fern in the United States, broad beech fern in Britain). One of the two beech ferns found growing in North America—*T. phegopteris* (northern beech fern) is the other. It is the largest and most erect, and grows naturally in sunny, open positions. It is considered hardy, but is deciduous in cold conditions.

T. noveboracensis (New York fern). A delicate and elegant looking fern from North America which spreads rapidly where it grows naturally—on the edges of marshes and in moist sunny clearings in woodlands. The fronds appear to grow in tufts of three or four together along a creeping rootstock. It is hardy but deciduous and tolerates high light conditions. Should be kept moist.

T. palustris (marsh fern—also known as *Dryopteris thelypteris*). This species is a dainty looking, but vigorous, invasive fern growing up to 1.5 m (5 ft) high. It is native to central Europe, India, China, Japan and central North America, where it grows naturally in marshes and on the edges of streams. It can be invasive in the garden. Enjoys a little lime in the soil. Keep it moist if planted in a pot and provide a large pot.

T. phegopteris (beech fern in Britain—also known as *Polypodium phegopteris, Dryopteris phegopteris*). This is a slow growing, hardy and deciduous species native to Europe, Asia and North America. It prefers shade and acid soil with the addition of leaf mould.

Left *Phyllitis scolopendrium,*
Right *Thelypteris phegopteris*

TODEA
(king fern in Australia)

A genus of two species of large terrestrial ferns which form a fibrous trunk with age and are topped by a number of

Thelypteris palustris

crowns of fronds. They are found in eastern Australia, New Zealand, Papua New Guinea and South Africa.

Todea barbara. A semi-hardy and adaptable fern that becomes tree-like and very handsome with age. The caudex may reach 1 to 1.5 m (4 to 5 ft) in height and 1 m (3 ft) in diameter. Multiple crowns may develop on the caudex so the plant can be quite massive. It will grow happily in an exposed situation where the fronds become broad and stunted, and in the shade, where the fronds elongate. Being so adaptable, the king fern makes an excellent potted plant in or out of doors. Planted directly into the ground, it should be given plenty of room to show itself off. The spores are short lived and should be sown while they are still fresh.

Todea barbara

WOODWARDIA
(chain fern in the United States and Britain)

A genus of easy to cultivate medium to large growing terrestrial ferns of coarse texture. The common name comes from the appearance of the sori, which are arranged in two precise rows on each side of the midrib of each frond. They are strong growing, woodland plants, appreciating moist, acid soil and tolerating some gentle sunlight.

Woodwardia radicans

W. radicans (European chain fern). A hardy, strong growing and easily cultivated fern from North America, southern Europe, Asia and the Atlantic Islands. The fronds, sometimes 2 m (6 ft) long, produce plantlets near to or at their tips. These grow quite large while still attached to the frond. This fern needs plenty of space so that its elegant arching shape can be appreciated. New fronds are pink, older fronds shades of pale green, and, during the winter months, mature fronds are purplish. One of the most colourful ferns, it is hardy, fast growing and tolerant of high light conditions, but it should be kept moist at all times.

WOODSIA

A genus of small alpine and woodland ferns found in circumpolar regions. Only a few of the rather rare species are cultivated.

Woodsia obtusa (blunt-lobed Woodsia). A small, hardy species that is easy to grow and especially suited to rock gardens or small pots. Found growing among limestone rocks in Britain and North America.

Tree ferns

Tree ferns are the diminutive descendants of the great ferns which, along with the giant mosses and horsetails, made up most of the world's vegetation in the Carboniferous era. The first of the vascular plants and hundreds of millions of years older than the seed bearing plants, their remains make up the coal seams that are to be found in today's warm temperate places.

They are generally tropical and warm temperate zone plants. Only a few that are native to the south-east corner of Australia and the continent of New Zealand will tolerate frost and prolonged cold. A tree fern with snow weighing down its fronds is a beautiful but rare sight.

Most ferns which form a trunk and carry their fronds in a whorl at the top are referred to as "tree ferns". Ferns with such growth habits are found in several genera including *Sadleria, Blechnum, Ctenitis, Cyathea, Dicksonia, Todea* and *Cibotium*. Under the tree fern heading only the commonly cultivated genera *Cibotium, Ctenitis, Cyathea* and *Dicksonia* are listed. Other cultivated ferns with a tree-like habit are the *Blechnum gibbum, Blechnum brasiliense* and *Todea barbara*. These are listed individually in the main fern list.

Recently there has been a great deal of confusion over the classification of tree ferns into appropriate genera. Some books list the commonly cultivated tree ferns under the genera *Sphaeropteris* and *Alsophila*; this book lists them under *Cyathea* and *Dicksonia* as these are names that are probably more familiar to most gardeners and have, so far, the longest standing. The genera *Cyathea* and *Dicksonia* have between them about 700 species but only a small portion (about 150 species) is cultivated.

CIBOTIUM

A genus of about 10 large growing tree ferns from Asia, Hawaii and the central Americas.

Cibotium glaucum (hapu, Hawaiian tree fern). A large semi-tender species whose fronds are carried high and tend to arch more gracefully than those of the *Cyathea* and *Dicksonia* species. The leaf bases and trunks are covered with tan silky hairs. It is not frequently cultivated beyond the warm areas of the west coast of America. It requires warmth, plenty of light and moist, humid conditions.

C. schiedei (Mexican tree fern). The gracefully arching fronds, caudex covered with lustrous yellow-brown hairs and white bloom on the undersides of the pale green fronds make this one of the most handsome species of the *Cibotium* genus. It is slow and low growing for many years and so makes an ideal tub plant. In its natural habitat it grows to about 4.5 m (15 ft). It is difficult to grow except in glasshouse conditions or mild areas.

CTENITIS

A genus of medium to large growing ferns from pantropic areas. Members of the genus are not often cultivated except by collectors.

Ctenitis sloanei (American tree fern, Florida tree fern). A large, tender species it is sometimes cultivated on the west coast of America.

CYATHEA

This is a complex genus consisting of about 800 species distributed widely throughout the warm temperate and tropical parts of the world. Generally the cultivated species listed below are hardy and vigorous plants that are suitable for pot cultivation while they are young and still relatively small. They need some protection from frost while young, but if fronds are damaged the plants recover quickly. Propagation by spores is easy. Species other than *C. australis* may be transplanted from the crown and upper part of the caudex without roots.

Cyathea australis

Cyathea cooperi

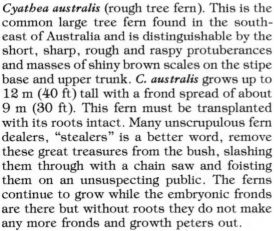

Cyathea australis (rough tree fern). This is the common large tree fern found in the south-east of Australia and is distinguishable by the short, sharp, rough and raspy protuberances and masses of shiny brown scales on the stipe base and upper trunk. *C. australis* grows up to 12 m (40 ft) tall with a frond spread of about 9 m (30 ft). This fern must be transplanted with its roots intact. Many unscrupulous fern dealers, "stealers" is a better word, remove these great treasures from the bush, slashing them through with a chain saw and foisting them on an unsuspecting public. The ferns continue to grow while the embryonic fronds are there but without roots they do not make any more fronds and growth peters out.

If planted correctly the rough tree fern is easily grown. It is a hardy variety, tolerating full sun if well watered.

C. baileyana (wig tree fern) This fern has a wig-like growth at the top of the trunk that is bright green when young and matures to a reddish-brown. Growing to a height of 5 m (17 ft) with a spread of 6 m (20 ft), it is a frost tender species.

C. cooperi (Australian tree fern). *C. cooperi* has a trunk patterned with clean-cut scars left by the fallen fronds. Its unfurling croziers are covered with long, silky white scales. This is a fast growing and hardy species reaching a height of about 12 metres (40 ft) with a spread of 12 metres.

C. cooperi var. *robusta* and *C. cooperi* var. *brentwood*. These are variants of the species which have been named in the United States. The coloration is their most distinguishing feature. The fronds of var. *robusta* are darker than those of the parent species while those of var. *brentwood* are a lighter green. The stipes of the species are pale green—var. *brentwood* has yellowish-green stipes and in var. *robusta* they are almost black. The trunks of the three ferns are also distinct. The species has the smallest trunk, var. *robusta*'s is slightly larger and var. *brentwood*'s is considerably larger. Both variants make good container plants and grow easily out of doors in warm temperate areas.

C. dealbata (ponga, silver king fern). A hardy tree fern whose fronds are New Zealand's national emblem. The fronds are silver underneath giving the plant its common name, but are delicate structures and need protection from the wind or they become very untidy. This species grows to 9 m (30 ft).

Cyathea dealbata

species distributed widely throughout the world. They are strange plants and considered rather primitive. The most graceful and hardy of the plants that are rather loosely called "tree ferns", they are not trees in any sense of the word. Others of the tree ferns at least have trunks; the "trunk" of these ferns, despite a height of sometimes 4.5 m (15 ft), consists entirely of a cluster of dead roots, dead butts and dead frond bases. These ferns are really epiphytes sitting on the top of an entwined, elongated mass of their own dead matter. The young roots must make their way down through this dead matter to find nourishment. In the wild the trunk is usually covered with epiphyte plants which trap humus and moisture along the way for the roots bound for the earth. The plants are really struggling unless the so-called trunk or root system is protected and kept moist—this is often an unsuspected cause of failure in cultivation. In the wild, too, Dicksonias that have fallen against others form great buttresses of roots all the way along their trunks, straight down to the ground below. This curtain of roots can be so dense that it is like coming up against a wall in the bush.

These lovely ferns should be planted where they can show off their great umbrella of arching fronds—plenty of space all the way round and filtered sunlight to keep the growth soft and green. At least one-third of the trunk should be planted in the ground so that the roots descending from the crown have not too far to grow to reach nourishment in their first few establishing months, and so that the plant is not continually rocked by wind and roots are not constantly dislodged. The trunk should be kept damp and the crown given some overhead protection in the first few months back in the ground. All species are easily raised from spores.

Dicksonia antarctica (soft tree fern). A hardy growing native of the eastern states of Australia and of Tasmania and a widely cultivated fern. The specimens growing in the northern extremities of the natural habitats are much less robust and much less common than are the Victorian and Tasmanian growing plants. This is the tree fern that is seen lying in forlorn heaps in nurseries shorn of its

C. medullaris (korau, mamaku, black tree fern). A species that is native to New Zealand and Polynesia and grows to 7.5 m (25 ft).

C. woollsiana. Found in northern Queensland's mountain areas, this is a lovely slender fern with broad arching fronds. It is hardy but grows best in the shade and is slightly frost tender. At maturity it can reach about 5 m (16 ft) with a frond span of 9 m (30 ft). It makes an excellent tub plant.

DICKSONIA

The Dicksonias are a commonly cultivated but relatively small genus of about 25

A Victorian photograph of a group of *Dicksonia antarctica* taken after a snow storm in Tasmania

fronds, with its trunk slashed through with a chain saw. It is amazing that it ever grows again! It does, and grows well, its fronds pushing up from the depths of the soft, hairy crown and new roots growing down the length of the caudex into the soil.

D. antarctica can grow to a height of 15 m (48 ft) with a frond span of 9 m (30 ft) —up to 40 fronds unfurl at a time, making a spectacular sight. It makes an ideal potted plant, happy for years in the same big tub, which is all the root space that it requires, and responding to regular feeding with leaf mould and bone meal. Pots should be well insulated or mulched as this fern must have plenty of water. This is the fern that is seen growing at the snow line. It is easily propagated from the spores and will, in congenial surroundings, self sow.

D. fibrosa (wheki-ponga). A slow growing New Zealand species closely allied to *D. antarctica*, but much less prickly, and smaller—2-6 m (6-20 ft). It is a hardy fern and grows well in conditions similar to those of the Australian variety, but it is not a very strong growing plant. Its true trunk is only 8-10 cm (3-4 in) in diameter, but covered in a mass of fibrous aerial roots several centimetres thick.

D. squarrosa (rough Dicksonia, wheki). A native of New Zealand, this species has a trunk reaching to 6 m (20 ft) and a crown of stiff, leathery, dark green fronds up to 2.5 m (8 ft) long. The trunk sometimes develops secondary growth below ground which produces runners and new growth if the main trunk is damaged. In the wild these runners form thickets of young ferns. An example of this growth is seen in the Ballarat Gardens in Victoria, where this fern has spread through the old fernery.

D. youngiae (bristly tree fern). A fast growing,

hardy and very pretty fern whose upper trunk and stipes are covered with stiff, reddish brown bristles. It comes from Queensland and northern New South Wales rainforest areas but is, however, rather rare. Offsets which form on the trunk can be removed with a sharp knife and potted, though they are slow to establish.

Filmy ferns

The filmy ferns are thought to be amongst the most primitive of living plants and form a quite distinctive, yet homogeneous, group within the fern family.

Their frond structure is only one cell thick, giving them their dainty, almost translucent quality and making them totally dependent on an extremely high humidity in their immediate atmosphere. Their dependence on atmospheric humidity suggests that they were one of the first vascular plants in the steamy jungles of ancient times.

The fragile structure of their fronds means that they are able to absorb moisture readily in a liquid or vapour form from the

Trichomanes radicans

large spore cases on vein endings at the margins of fronds is distinct and less complicated than that of other ferns.

Trichomanes reniforme

atmosphere around them, and means, too, that they lose moisture readily so that they quickly become a dehydrated shrivelled mass if they are without this moisture for too long.

Botanically they are interesting plants. The method by which they carry their

The filmy ferns are hard to cultivate in the open garden unless there are dripping rock crevices or a naturally sheltered, moist situation. The ordinary glasshouse, too, is often too arid for these demanding ferns and they can only be grown to look their luxurious best if partially enclosed in a shaded part of the house. If the walls of the enclosure are lined with moss and the whole kept constantly moist by seeping water, or by means of a humidifier (so that humidity is almost 100 per cent), the plants can be grown directly on the moss or in pots buried in the moss. They will grow well under these conditions if their demands for moderate temperatures, good drainage and low, indirect light are also met.

The commonly cultivated genera *Hymenophyllum*, *Mecodium* and *Trichomanes* make ideal plants for a terrarium where the atmosphere can be maintained at almost dewpoint, but should not be mixed with other plants as their roots form a dense, over-whelming mass.

Trichomanes angustatum

Aquatic ferns

The two most frequently cultivated aquatic fern genera, *Azolla* and *Marsilea*, are often dismissed as fern oddities because of their distinctly unfern-like appearance, but their look is deceptive for they are true ferns in their structure and reproductive ways. *Ceratopteris*, another genus of cultivated aquatic ferns, is more fern-like.

AZOLLA

A small genus of floating aquatic ferns which spread rapidly over large areas of still or gently moving water by means of self division; the six or so species are widely spread throughout the world. Despite tiny leaves and dainty appearance the species are hardy and strong growing and will often over-whelm other aquatic plants. The Azollas will recover quickly even if removed in handfuls from ornamental ponds. At certain times of the year the fronds take on a distinct rusty red hue which is a pleasant contrast to the bright green of most other water dwelling plants. All species live in a symbiotic relation-ship with a blue-green alga called *Anabaena azolla*, which lives in pouches on the ferns' leaves. All grow easily in pools and dams in sunlight or shade. A little fertiliser added to the water greatly assists their growth.

CERATOPTERIS

A genus of two species of aquatic, dimorphic ferns from South-East Asia. *Ceratopteris thalictroides* (water fern). A fragile, light green fern that grows in mud or completely submerged in water. The fertile fronds as well as producing spores bear plant-lets which, when mature, float away from the parent to form new plants. It is easily grown in ponds in warm temperate areas and with protection in cool temperate areas. Makes a good aquarium plant. The fern is edible.

Ceratopteris thalictroides

MARSILEA

(individual specimens are commonly called nardoos)

A genus of about 60 species of most unfern-like aquatic ferns that in fact look more like floating four-leaved clover, covered with silky hairs. Their method of reproduction is very sophisticated for the fern family, and is very close to that of flowering plants. The spores form in cases called sporocarps, carried at the bottom of the short stipes. Two different types of spores are produced — megaspores, which germinate into prothalli bearing archegonia or female reproductive organs, and microspores, which germinate into prothalli bearing antheridia or male reproductive organs.

The nardoos are easily grown in sheltered boggy places on the edges of ponds or in wide, shallow pots kept constantly moist.

Fern allies and masqueraders

Fern allies make up a very ancient group of plants which developed and reached their peak in the Carboniferous era. They are commonly known as horsetails (Class Sphenopsida), clubmosses (Class Lycopodida, the most primitive of the classes of fern allies), quillworts and whisk ferns (Class Psiloptopsida).

Like true ferns the fern allies reproduce by means of spores, but unlike them they do not produce a true frond, but a much simpler and smaller leaf borne on flattened branches. Another important difference is that the fern allies carry their spores in cases between the leaves and crowded into club-like cones (called strobili)—in the true ferns the spore cases are carried on the underside or edges of the fronds.

The most commonly cultivated fern allies are the genera *Lycopodium* and *Selaginella*, both belonging to the Class Lycopida, which are closely related.

The Selaginellas, commonly called clubmosses, make up a large genus of about 600 species found throughout the world. They are generally small plants of soft, mossy or fern-like appearance and are hardy and tolerant of low light conditions, though humidity should be kept high to maintain an attractive look. Their low growing habit makes them useful as a ground cover in cool, damp places. They make pretty individual potted plants or combine well with tall arching ferns in a hanging basket, quickly covering bare bark, moss and wire with a delicate green fuzz. Humidity must be adequate and soil kept moist.

The commonly named tassel ferns make up a distinct group within the *Lycopodium* genus. They are epiphytes which have long pendulous stems bearing crowded scale-like leaves and, at their tips, long clubs hanging in tassels. They make ideal ferns for hanging baskets, but because of their tropical origins must be in a protected position even in warm areas and be given glass protection in less temperate areas. The fronds are delicate and need protection from the sun and wind.

As for the fern masqueraders they must be mentioned here because of the brazen way they have very successfully posed as their beautiful cousins. They are often graced with the title "fern", and must be exposed for what they are!

Many plants imitate the fern, but none so successfully as some members of the *Asparagus* genus —a genus of about 100 species belonging to the lily family. They come from South Africa and were first collected at the end of the nineteenth century. *A. plumosa* is the species with the soft feathery fronds and the one most often mistaken for a fern. It will climb in a scrambling sort of way in a sheltered place outside. *A. sprengerii* is the bushy plant whose fronds elongate in low light conditions in a fair imitation of one of the *Nephrolepis* species. Both these *Asparagus* species are hardy plants tolerating low temperatures and quite shady positions. They prefer a confined root space and should never be allowed to dry out. Unlike ferns, they are prickly to the touch.

GLOSSARY

ANTHERIDIUM — The part of the prothallus containing the sperm-producing male sexual organ. Plural *ANTHERIDIA*.

APOGAMY — The production of a sporophyte from the tissues of the prothallus without the normal fertilisation process.

APOSPORY — The production of a prothallus on the tissues of a sporophyte without the normal fertilisation process.

ARCHEGONIUM — The part of the prothallus containing the egg-producing female organ. Plural *ARCHEGONIA*.

BULBIL — A small bulb-like bud which is borne on a frond and develops into a plantlet.

CAUDEX — The trunk of a tree fern and correctly, though not often used, any small erect fern rhizome.

CROZIER — An uncoiled young frond.

CULTIVAR — A plant variety developed under cultivation.

DIMORPHIC — Bearing two types of fronds, usually one fertile and the other sterile.

EPIPHYTE — A plant which grows on another for support — not a parasite.

FALSE INDUSIUM — A spore case covering formed by a reflexed leaf margin.

FERN ALLIES — Relatives of ferns which reproduce by means of spores but which have a much simpler tissue structure.

FERTILE — Used in reference to fronds, meaning those which carry spores.

FORM — A botanical division below a species. Plural *FORMA*.

FRIABLE — Soil which is loose in texture.

FROND — The part of a fern called a leaf in other plants.

GENUS — A botanical division which groups related species. Plural *GENERA*.

GAMETOPHYTE — A small, flat plant bearing the reproductive organs, i.e. the prothallus.

GLAUCOUS — A covering bloom giving a blue tinge to the tissues.

HYBRID — A plant resulting from the crossing of two plants of different characteristics.

INDUSIUM — The membrane covering the sorus or cluster of spore cases.

LITHOPHYTE — A plant that grows on rocks.

MUTATION	A sudden change in plants and animals due to changes in the genes or chromosomes. The changes can be inherited by future generations.	**SORUS**	A cluster of spore cases. Plural *SORI*.
		SPORANGIUM	The capsule containing the spores. Plural *SPORANGIA*.
PINNA	The primary segment of the divided frond.	**SPORE**	The dust-like cell which germinates into the prothallus.
PINNULE	The secondary pinna.		
PROLIFEROUS	The vegetative production rather than the sexual reproduction of new plants.	**SPORELINGS**	A young fern which has developed from a prothallus.
		SPOROPHYTE	The asexual fern generation or spore bearing plant as opposed to the gametophyte or prothallus.
PROTHALLUS	The tiny flat plant which grows from a spore and carries the reproductive organs. Plural *PROTHALLI*.		
		STIPE	The stalk of the frond from the rhizome to the leaf blade.
PUPS	The common name given to new plants which form on species of *Platycerium*.	**STOLON**	A stem capable of producing a new plant at its tip.
RACHIS	The midrib of a frond.		
RHIZOME	The stem which produces roots and grows horizontally above or below ground, or grows vertically as in climbing and tree ferns.	**SYNONYM**	An alternate, but not necessarily correct, scientific name.
		TERRESTRIAL	A botanical term describing a plant that grows on the ground.
ROOTSTOCK	The part of the stem which is underground and to which the roots are attached.	**VARIETY**	A botanical division below a species but above a form.
SCALES	Small, flat, papery structures borne on stems and rhizomes.	**XEROPHYTE**	A plant adapted to dry conditions.

INDEX

Page references in bold type indicate main entry

INDEX